P9-EEG-764

The TRAGEDY
of the EURO

PHILIPP BAGUS

SECOND EDITION

MISES
INSTITUTE

© 2010 Ludwig von Mises Institute
© 2011 Terra Libertas
© 2012 Ludwig von Mises Institute

Ludwig von Mises Institute
518 West Magnolia Avenue
Auburn, Alabama, 36832, U.S.A.
Mises.org

ISBN: 978-1-61016-249-4

The TRAGEDY
of the EURO

To Eva

Contents

Graphs

Tables

Acknowledgments

I would like to thank Daniel Ajamian, Brecht Arnaert, Philip Booth, Brian Canny, Nikolay Gertchev, Robert Grözinger, Guido Hülsmann, and Robin Michaels for helpful comments and suggestions on an earlier draft, Arlene Oost-Zinner for careful editing, and Jesús Huerta de Soto for writing the foreword. All remaining errors are my own.

Foreword

by Jesús Huerta de Soto

It is a great pleasure for me to present this book by my colleague Philipp Bagus, one of my most brilliant and promising students. The book is extremely timely and shows how the interventionist setup of the European Monetary system has led to disaster.

The current sovereign debt crisis is the direct result of credit expansion by the European banking system. In the early 2000s, credit was expanded especially in the periphery of the European Monetary Union such as in Ireland, Greece, Portugal, and Spain. Interest rates were reduced substantially by credit expansion coupled with a fall both in inflationary expectations and risk premiums. The sharp fall in inflationary expectations was caused by the prestige of the newly created European Central Bank as a copy of the Bundesbank. Risk premiums were reduced artificially due to the expected support by stronger nations. The result was an artificial boom. Asset price bubbles such as a housing bubble in Spain developed. The newly created money was primarily injected in the countries of the periphery where it financed overconsumption and malinvestments, mainly in an overextended automobile and construction sector. At the same time, the credit expansion also helped to finance and expand unsustainable welfare states.

In 2007, the microeconomic effects that reverse any artificial boom financed by credit expansion and not by genuine real savings started to show up. Prices of means of production such as commodities and wages rose. Interest rates also climbed due to inflationary pressure that made central banks reduce their expansionary stands. Finally, consumer goods prices started to rise relative to the prices offered to the originary factors of productions. It became more and more obvious that many investments were not sustainable due to a lack of real savings. Many of these investments occurred in the construction sector. The financial sector came under pressure as mortgages had been securitized, ending up directly or indirectly on balance sheets of financial institutions. The pressures culminated in the collapse of the investment bank Lehman Brothers, which led to a full-fledged panic in financial markets.

Instead of letting market forces run their course, governments unfortunately intervened with the necessary adjustment process. It is this unfortunate intervention that not only prevented a faster and more thorough recovery, but also produced, as a side effect, the sovereign debt crisis of spring 2010. Governments tried to prop up the overextended sectors, increasing their spending. They paid subsidies for new car purchases to support the automobile industry and started public works to support the construction sector as well as the sector that had lent to these industries, the banking sector. Moreover, governments supported the financial sector directly by giving guarantees on their liabilities, nationalizing banks, buying their assets or partial stakes in them. At the same time, unemployment soared due to regulated labor markets. Governments' revenues out of income taxes and social security plummeted. Expenditures for unemployment subsidies increased. Corporate taxes that had been inflated artificially in sectors like banking, construction, and car manufacturing during the boom were almost completely wiped out. With falling revenues and increasing expenditures governments' deficits and debts soared, as a direct consequence of governments' responses to the crisis caused by a boom that was not sustained by real savings.

The case of Spain is paradigmatic. The Spanish government subsidized the car industry, the construction sector, and the banking industry, which had been expanding heavily during the credit expansion of the boom. At the same time a very inflexible labor market caused official unemployment rates to rise to twenty percent. The resulting public deficit began to frighten markets and fellow EU member states, which finally pressured the government to announce some timid austerity measures in order to be able to keep borrowing.

In this regard, the single currency showed one of its "advantages." Without the Euro, the Spanish government would have most certainly devalued its currency as it did in 1993, printing money to reduce its deficit. This would have implied a revolution in the price structure and an immediate impoverishment of the Spanish population as import prices would have soared. Furthermore, by devaluating, the government could have continued its spending without any structural reforms. With the Euro, the Spanish (or any other troubled government) cannot devalue or print its currency directly to pay off its debt. Now these governments had to engage in austerity measures and some structural reforms after pressure by the Commission and member states like Germany. Thus, it is possible that the second scenario for the future as mentioned by Philipp Bagus in the present book will play out. The Stability and Growth Pact might be reformed and enforced. As a consequence, the governments of the European Monetary Union would have to continue and intensify their austerity measures and structural reforms in order to comply with the Stability and Growth Pact. Pressured by conservative countries like Germany, all of the European Monetary Union would follow the path of traditional crisis policies with spending cuts.

In contrast to the EMU, the United States follows the Keynesian recipe for recessions. In the Keynesian view, during a crisis the government has to substitute a fall in "aggregate demand" by increasing its spending. Thus, the US engages in deficit spending and extremely expansive monetary policies to "jump start" the economy. Maybe one of the beneficial effects of the Euro has been to push all of the EMU toward the path of austerity. In fact, I have argued before that the single currency is a step in the right direction as it fixes exchange rates in Europe and thereby ends monetary nationalism and the chaos of flexible fiat exchange rates manipulated by governments, especially, in times of crisis.

My dear colleague Philipp Bagus has challenged me on my rather positive view on the Euro from the time when he was a student in my class, pointing correctly to the advantages of currency competition. His book, *The Tragedy of the Euro*, may be read as an elaborated exposition of his arguments against the Euro. While the single currency does away with monetary nationalism in Europe from a theoretical point of view, the question is: just how stable is the single currency in actuality? Bagus deals with this question from two angles, providing at the same time the two main achievements and contributions of the book: a historical analysis of the origins of the Euro and a theoretical analysis of the workings and mechanisms of the Eurosystem. Both analyses point in the same direction. In the historical analysis, Bagus deals with the origins of the Euro and the ECB. He uncovers the interests of national governments, politicians and bankers in a similar way that Rothbard does in relation to the origin of the Federal Reserve System in *The Case against the Fed*. In fact, the book could also have been analogously titled *The Case against the ECB*. Considering the political interests, dynamics and circumstances that led to the introduction of the Euro, it becomes clear that the Euro might in fact be a step in the wrong direction; a step toward a pan-European inflationary fiat currency aimed to push aside limits that competition and the conservative monetary policy of the Bundesbank had imposed before. Bagus's theoretical analysis makes the inflationary purpose and setup of the Eurosystem even clearer. The Eurosystem is unmasked as a self-destroying system that leads to massive redistribution across the EMU, with incentives for governments to use the ECB as a device to finance their deficits. He shows that the concept of the Tragedy of the Commons, which I have applied to the case of fractional reserve banking, is also applicable to the Eurosystem, where different European governments can exploit the value of the single currency.

I am glad that this book is being made available to the public by the Mises Institute and Terra Libertas Publishing

House. The future of Europe and the world depends on the understanding of the monetary theory and the workings of monetary institutions. This book provides strong tools toward understanding the history of the Euro and its perverse institutional setup. Hopefully, it can help to turn the tide toward a sound monetary system in Europe and worldwide.

Introduction

The recent crisis of the Eurosystem has shaken financial markets and governments. The Euro has depreciated strongly against other currencies at a pace worrisome to political and financial elites. They fear losing control. The monthly bulletin of the European Central Bank (ECB), published in June of 2010, acknowledges that the European banking system was on the brink of collapse in the beginning of May. Several European governments, including France, were on the verge of default. In fact, default risks for some European banks, as measured by credit default swaps, surged to higher levels than they did during the panics that followed the collapse of Lehman Brothers in September of 2008.

In reaction to the crisis, the political class has tried desperately to save the socialist project of a common fiat currency for Europe. They have been successful—at least for the time being. After intense negotiations, an unprecedented €750 billion "rescue parachute" has been created to support European governments and banks. At the same time, however, the ECB has started what many had regarded as unthinkable before: the outright purchase of government bonds, an action which undermines its credibility and independence.[1] The public and market perception of the monetary setup of the European Monetary Union (EMU) will never be the same.

---

[1] Roughly a year before starting to purchase government bonds, the ECB started to buy covered bonds issued by German banks. The purchases were progressive and reached €60 billion.

Resistance to these unprecedented measures is on the rise, especially in countries with traditionally conservative monetary and budget policies. A poll in Germany showed that fifty-six percent of Germans were against the bailout fund.[2]

It is not surprising that the majority of Germans want to return to the Deutschmark.[3] They seem to understand intuitively that they are at the losing end of a complex system. They see that they are saving and tightening their belts on a regular basis while other countries' governments embark on wild spending sprees. A prime illustration is the "Tourism for All" programme in Greece: the poor receive government funds toward vacations. Even amid the crisis, the Greek government continues the programme, albeit reducing the number of subsidized vacation nights to two.[4] The Greek government also upholds a more generous public pension system than Germany does. Greek workers get a pension of up to eighty percent of their average wages. German workers get only forty-six percent, a number that will fall to forty-two percent in the future. While Greeks get fourteen pension payments per year, Germans receive twelve.[5]

Germans assess the bailout of Greece as a rip off. The bailout makes the involuntary transfers embedded in the EMU more obvious. But most people still do not understand exactly how and why they pay. They suspect that the Euro has something to do with it.

The project of the Euro has been pushed by European socialists to enhance their dream of a central European state. But the project is about to fail. The collapse is far from being a

---

[2] Cash-online, "Forsa: Deutsche überwiegend gegen den Euro-Rettungsschirm." News from June 7, 2010, http://www.cash-online.de.

[3] Shortnews.de, "Umfrage: Mehr als die Hälfte der Deutschen wollen die DM zurück haben." News from June 29, 2010, http://shortnews.de.

[4] GRReporter, "The Social Tourism of Bankrupt Greece," July 12, 2010, http://www.grreporter.info. In the summer of 2010, many Greek entrepreneurs did not want to serve clients participating in the state programme. The Greek government pays its bills six months late, if at all.

[5] D. Hoeren and O. Santen, "Griechenland-Pleite: Warum zahlen wir ihre Luxus-Renten mit Milliarden-Hilfe?" *bild-online.de*, April 27, 2010, http://bild.de.

coincidence. It is already implied in the institutional setup of the EMU, whose evolution we will trace in this book. The story is one of intrigue, and economic and political interests. It is fascinating story in which politicians fight for power, influence and their own egos.

CHAPTER ONE

Two Visions for Europe

There has been a fight between the advocates of two differ-ent ideals from the beginning of the European Union. Which stance should it adopt: the classical liberal vision, or the socialist vision of Europe? The introduction of the Euro has played a key role in the strategies of these two visions.[1] In order to understand the tragedy of the Euro and its history, it is important to be fa-miliar with these two diverging, and underlying visions and ten-sions that have come to the fore in the face of a single currency.

THE CLASSICAL LIBERAL VISION

The founding fathers of the EU, Schuman (France [born in Luxembourg]), Adenauer (Germany), and Alcide de Gas-peri (Italy), all German speaking Catholics, were closer to the classical liberal vision of Europe.[2] They were also Christian

---

[1] See Jesús Huerta de Soto, "Por una Europa libre," in *Nuevos Estudios de Eco-nomía Política* (2005), pp. 214–216. See Hans Albin Larsson, "National Policy in Disguise: A Historical Interpretation of the EMU," in *The Price of the Euro*, ed. Jonas Ljundberg (New York: Palgrave MacMillan, 2004), pp. 143–170, on the two alternatives for Europe.

[2] Another important defender of this vision was the German politician Lud-wig Erhard, father of the Wirtschaftswunder. Erhard criticized intentions to introduce "planification" for Europe. See Ludwig Erhard "Planification—kein Modell für Europa," in: Karl Hohmann (ed.), *Ludwig Erhard. Gedanken aus fünf Jahrzehnten*, Düsseldorf: ECON, pp. 770–780. Erhard even criticized

democrats. The classical liberal vision regards individual liberty as the most important cultural value of Europeans and Christianity. In this vision sovereign European states defend private property rights and a free market economy in a Europe of open borders, thus enabling the free exchange of goods, services and ideas.

The Treaty of Rome in 1957 was the main achievement toward the classical liberal vision for Europe. The Treaty delivered four basic liberties: free circulation of goods, free offering of services, free movement of financial capital, and free migration. The Treaty restored rights that had been essential for Europe during the classical liberal time in the nineteenth century, but had been abandoned in the age of nationalism and socialism. The Treaty was a turning away from the age of socialism that had lead to conflicts between European nations, culminating in two world wars.

The classical liberal vision aims at a restoration of nineteenth century freedoms. Free competition without entry barriers should prevail in a common European market. In this vision, no one could prohibit a German hairdresser from cutting hair in Spain, and no one could tax an English man for transferring money from a German to a French bank, or for investing in the Italian stock market. No one could prevent, through regulations, a French brewer from selling beer in Germany. No government could give subsidies distorting competition. No one could prevent a Dane from running away from his welfare state and extreme high tax rates, and migrating to a state with a lower tax burden, such as Ireland.

---

the Treaty of Rome for its interventionist components. He and other Germans regarded the European project as neo-mercantilist. See Michael Wohlgemuth, "Europäische Ordnungspolitik, Anmerkungen aus ordnungs- und konstitutionenökonomischer Sicht," in *ORDO: Jahrbuch für Ordnung von Wirtschaft und Gesellschaft,* (2008), pp. 381–340. A theoretical foundation for the classical liberal vision is spelt out in Hans Sennholz, *How can Europe Survive* (New York: D. Van Nostrand Company, 1955). Sennholz criticizes the plans for government cooperation brought forwards by different politicians and shows that only freedom eliminates the cause of conflicts in Europe. For the importance of catholic political leaders in forming the Common Market during the early years of European integration see "Catholicism Growing Strong in Europe," *Irish Independent,* October 28, 1959.

In order to accomplish this ideal of peaceful cooperation and flourishing exchanges, nothing more than freedom would be necessary. In this vision there would be no need to create a European superstate. In fact, the classical liberal vision is highly sceptical of a central European state; it is considered detrimental to individual liberty. Philosophically speaking, many defenders of this vision are inspired by Catholicism, and borders of the European community are defined by Christianity. In line with Catholic social teaching, a principle of subsidiarity should prevail: problems should be solved at the lowest and least concentrated level possible. The only centralized European institution acceptable would be a European Court of Justice, its activities restricted to supervising conflicts between member states, and guaranteeing the four basic liberties.

From the classical liberal point of view, there should be many competing political systems, as has been the case in Europe of centuries. In the Middle Ages and until the nineteenth century, there existed very different political systems, such as independent cities of Flanders, Germany and Northern Italy. There were Kingdoms such as Bavaria or Saxony, and there were Republics such as Venice. Political diversity was demonstrated most clearly in the strongly decentralized Germany. Under a culture of diversity and pluralism, science and industry flourished.[3]

Competition on all levels is essential to the classical liberal vision. It leads to coherence, as product standards, factor prices, and especially wage rates tend to converge. Capital moves there, where wages are low, bidding them up; workers, on the other hand move where wage rates are high, bidding them down. Markets offer decentralized solutions for environmental problems based on private property. Political competition ensures the most important European value: liberty. Tax competition fosters lower

---

[3] Roland Vaubel, "The Role of Competition in the Rise of Baroque and Renaissance Music," *Journal of Cultural Economics* 25 (2005): pp. 277–297, argues that the rise of Baroque and Renaissance music in Germany and Italy resulted from the decentralization of these countries and the resulting competition.

tax rates and fiscal responsibility. People vote by foot, evading excessive tax rates, as do companies. Different national tax sovereignties are seen as the best protection against tyranny. Competition also prevails in the field of money. Different monetary authorities compete in offering currencies of high quality. Authorities offering more stable currencies exert pressure on other authorities to follow suit.

THE SOCIALIST VISION

In direct opposition to the classical liberal vision is the socialist or Empire vision of Europe, defended by politicians such as Jacques Delors or François Mitterrand. A coalition of statist interests of the nationalist, socialist, and conservative ilk does what it can do to advance its agenda. It wants to see the European Union as an empire or a fortress: protectionist to the outside and interventionist on the inside. These statists dream of a centralized state with efficient technocrats—as the ruling technocrat statists imagine themselves to be—managing it.

In this ideal, the centre of the Empire would rule over the periphery. There would be common and centralized legislation. The defenders of the socialist vision of Europe want to erect a European mega state reproducing the nation states on the European level. They want a European welfare state that would provide for redistribution, regulation, and harmonization of legislation within Europe. The harmonization of taxes and social regulations would be carried out at the highest level. If the VAT is between twenty-five and fifteen percent in the European Union, socialists would harmonize it to twenty-five percent in all countries. Such harmonization of social regulation is in the interest of the most protected, the richest and the most productive workers, who can "afford" such regulation—while their peers cannot. If German social regulations would be applied to the Poles, for instance, the latter would have problems competing with the former.

The agenda of the socialist vision is to grant ever more power to the central state, i.e., to Brussels. The socialist vision for Europe is the ideal of the political class, the bureaucrats, the interest groups, the privileged, and the subsidized sectors who want to create a powerful central state for their own enrichment. Adherents to this view present a European state as a necessity, and consider it only a question of time.

Along the socialist path, the European central state would one day become so powerful that the sovereign states would become subservient to it. (We can already see first indicators of such subservience in the case of Greece and Ireland. Both countries behave like protectorates of Brussels, who tells the governments how to handle their deficits.)

The socialist vision provides no obvious geographical limits for the European state—in contrast to the Catholic inspired classical liberal vision. Political competition is seen as an obstacle to the central state, which removes itself from public control. In this sense the central state in the socialist vision becomes less and less democratic as power is shifted to bureaucrats and technocrats. (An example is provided by the European Commission, the executive body of the European Union. The Commissioners are not elected but appointed by the member state governments.)

Historically, precedents for this old socialist plan of founding a controlling central state in Europe were established by Charlemagne, Napoleon, Stalin and Hitler. The difference is, however, that this time no direct military means would be necessary. But state power coercion is used in the push for a central European state.

From a tactical perspective, crisis situations in particular would be used by the adherents of the socialist vision to create new institutions (such as the European Central Bank—ECB— or possibly, in the future, a European Ministry of Finance), as well as to extend the powers of existing institutions such as the European Commission or the ECB.[4, 5]

---

[4] On the tendency of states to expand their power in emergency situations see Robert Higgs, *Crisis and Leviathan: Critical Episodes in the Growth of American Government* (Oxford: Oxford University Press, 1987).

[5] Along these lines, French President Nicolas Sarkozy tried to introduce a European rescue fund during the crisis of 2008 (see Patrick Hosking, "France Seeks €300 billion Rescue Fund for Europe." *Timesonline*. October 2, 2008, http://business.timesonline.co.uk). German chancellor Angela Merkel resisted,

The classical liberal and the socialist visions of Europe are, consequently, irreconcilable. In fact, the increase in power of a central state as proposed by the socialist vision implies a reduction of the four basic liberties, and most certainly less individual liberty.

THE HISTORY OF A STRUGGLE
BETWEEN TWO VISIONS

The two visions have been struggling with each other since the 1950s. In the beginning, the design for the European Communities adhered more closely to the classical liberal vision.[6] The European Community consisted of sovereign states and guaranteed the four basic liberties. From the point of view of the classical liberals, a main birth defect of the community was the subsidy and intervention in agricultural policy. Also, by construction, the only legislative initiative belongs to the European

---

however, and became known as "Madame Non." The recent crisis was also used by the ECB to extend its operations and balance sheet. Additional institutions, such as the European Systemic Risk Board or the European Financial Stability Facility [(EFSF) – to be followed by the European Stability Mechanism (ESM)], were established during the crisis.

[6] The European Communities consisted of the European Coal and Steel Community, creating a common market for coal and steel; the European Economic Community (EEC), advancing economic integration; and the European Atomic Energy Community, creating a specialist market for nuclear power and distributing it through the Community. Yet, even at the very beginning of European integration we can already appreciate the "socialist intentions" of Jean Monnet, the French intellectual father of the European Community. Monnet planned the European Community to be a supra-national rather than an inter-governmental organization [Christopher Booker and Richard North, *The Great Deception: Can the European Union Survive?* (London: Continuum, 2005)]. For Monnet's tendency toward central planning see also Tony Judt, *Postwar: A History of Europe since 1945* (London: Vintage, 2010, p. 70). The French government feared a German revival after World War II. The EEC assured the French privileged access to German resources (Judt, *Postwar*, p. 117). The integration of Germany into Europe was thought to prevent a German revolt against the conditions imposed upon it after the war. As Judt, *Postwar*, p. 156, writes: "[The High Authority of the EEC] above all would take control of the Ruhr and other vital German resources out of purely German hands. It represented a European solution to a—*the*—French problem." Despite these political intentions behind the EEC, elements of the classical liberal tradition remained strong in the beginning.

Commission. Once the Commission has made a proposal for legislation, the Council of the European Union alone, or together with the European Parliament, may approve the proposal.[7] This setup contains the seed of centralization. Consequently, the institutional setup, from the very beginning, was designed to accommodate centralization and dictatorship over minority opinions, as unanimity is not required for all decisions and the areas were unanimity rule is required have been reduced over the years.[8]

The classical liberal model is defended traditionally by Christian democrats and states such as the Netherlands, Germany, and also Great Britain.[9] But social democrats and socialists, usually led by the French government, defend the Empire version of Europe. In fact, in light of its rapid fall in 1940, the years of Nazi occupation, its failures in Indochina, and the loss of its African colonies, the French ruling class used the European Community to regain its influence and pride, and to compensate for the loss of its empire.[10]

---

[7] The Council of the European Union, often referred to as the "Council" or "Council of Ministers," is constituted by one minister of each member state and should not be confused with the European Council. The European Council is composed of the President of the "Council of Ministers," the President of the Commission, and one representative per member state. The European Council gives direction to the EU by defining the policy agenda.

[8] These important birth defects reduce the credit given to the founding fathers such as Schuman, Adenauer and others.

[9] In 1959, for instance, the British government suggested a free trade zone for all of non-communist Europe. The proposal was rejected by Charles de Gaulle.

[10] Larsson, "National Policy in Disguise," p. 162. As Larsson writes: "The arena, in which France sought to recreate its honor and international influence was that of Western Europe. As the leading country in the EEC, France regained influence to compensate for the loss of its empire, and within an area where France, traditionally and in different ways, had sought to dominate and influence." As Judt, *Postwar*, p. 153 writes: "Unhappy and frustrated at being reduced to the least of the great powers, France had embarked upon a novel vocation as the initiator of a new Europe." "For Charles de Gaulle, the lesson of the twentieth century was that France could only hope to recover its lost glories by investing in the European project and shaping it into the service of French goals." (p. 292) Already in 1950 the French premier, René Pleven, proposed to create a European Army as part of a European Defence Community (under the leadership of France). Even though the plan ultimately failed, it provides evidence that from the very beginning, French politicians

Over the years there has been a slow tendency toward the socialist ideal—with increasing budgets for the EU and a new regional policy that effectively redistributes wealth across Europe.[11] Countless regulations and harmonization have pushed in that direction as well.

The classical liberal vision of sovereign and independent states did appear to be given new strength by the collapse of the Soviet Union and the reunification of Germany. First, Germany, having traditionally defended this vision, became stronger due to the reunification. Second, the new states emerging from the ashes of communism, such as Czechoslovakia (Václav Klaus), Poland, Hungary, etc., also supported the classical liberal vision for Europe. These new states wanted to enjoy their new, recently won liberty. They had had enough of socialism, Empires, and centralization.

The influence of the French government was now reduced.[12] The socialist camp saw its defeat coming. A fast enlargement of the EU incorporating the new states in the East had to be prevented. A step toward a central state had to be taken. The single

---

pushed for centralization and the empire vision of Europe. An exception is French President Charles de Gaulle, who opposed a supranational European state. During the "empty chair crisis" France abandoned its seat in the Council of Ministers for six months in June 1965 in protest against an attack on its sovereignty. The Commission had pushed for a centralization of power. Yet, de Gaulle was also trying to improve the French position and leadership in the negotiations over the Common Agricultural Policy. The Commission had proposed majority voting in this area. French farmers were the main beneficiaries of the subsidies while Germany was the main contributor. Majority voting could have deprived French farmers of their privileges. Only when de Gaulle's agricultural funding demands were accepted the policy of the empty chair ended. Many Germans including Ludwig Erhard opposed the agricultural subsidies and favored a free trade zone. (See Judt, *Postwar*, p. 304). Adenauer, however, would never break with France. In exchange for subsidies for French farmers, German goods gained free entry into France. It was agricultural subsidies in exchange for free trade.

[11] Roland Vaubel, "The Political Economy of Centralization and the European Community," *Public Choice* 81 (1–2 1994): pp. 151–190, explains the trend toward centralization in Europe with public choice arguments.

[12] Larsson, "National Policy in Disguise," p. 163.

currency was to be the vehicle to achieve this aim.[13] According to the German newspapers, the French government feared that Germany, after its reunification, would create "a DM dominated free trade area from Brest to Brest-Litowsk."[14] European (French) socialists needed power over the monetary unit urgently.

As Charles Gave[15] argued on the events following the fall of the Berlin wall:

> For the proponents of the "Roman Empire" [socialist vision], the European State had to be organized immediately, whatever the risks, and become inevitable. Otherwise, the proponents of "Christian Europe" [classical liberal vision] would win by default and history would likely never reverse its course. The collapse of the Soviet

---

[13] As Arjen Klamer, "Borders Matter: Why the Euro is a Mistake and Why it will Fail," in *The Price of the Euro*, ed. Jonas Ljundberg, (New York: Palgrave MacMillan, 2004), p. 33, writes on the strategy of using the single currency as a vehicle for centralization: "The presumption was that once the monetary union was a fact, a kind of federal construction or at least a closer political union, would have to follow in order to make the monetary union work. Thus, the wagon was put in front of the horse. It was an experiment. No politician dared to face the question of what the consequences would be of failure, or of that would happen if a strong political union did not come about. The train had to go on."

Similarly Roland Vaubel, "A Critical Analysis of EMU and of Sweden Joining It," in *The Price of the Euro*, ed. Jonas Ljundberg, (New York: Palgrave MacMillan 2004), p. 94, writes on the effects of the Euro: "European Monetary Union is the stepping stone for the centralization of many other economic policies and, ultimately, for the founding of a European state." See also James Foreman-Peck, "The UK and the Euro: Politics versus Economics in a Long-Run Perspective," in *The Price of the Euro*, ed. Jonas Ljundberg, (New York: Palgrave MacMillan, 2004), p. 104.

[14] *Frankfurter Allgemeine Zeitung*, June 1, 1996. German Foreign Minister Hans-Dietrich Genscher had proposed to absorb the Eastern European countries into the EU as fast as possible. Margaret Thatcher also called for a fast enlargement with the hope that the enlarged EU would turn into a free trade area. Fearing a free trade area and a diminishing influence, the French government opposed the early access of Eastern European countries into the EU. See Judt, *Postwar*, pp. 716, 719.

[15] Charles Gave, "Was the Demise of the USSR a Negative Event?" in *Investors-Insight.com*, ed. John Mauldin, (May 5, 2010), http://investorsinsight.com.

Union was the crisis which gave the opportunity, and drive, to the Roman Empire to push through an overly ambitious program. The scale had been tipped and the "Roman Empire" needed to tip it the other way; and the creation of the Euro, more than anything, came to symbolize the push by the Roman camp toward a centralized super-structure.

The official line of argument for the defenders of a single fiat currency was that the Euro would lower transactions costs—facilitating trade, tourism and growth in Europe. More implicitly, however, the single currency was seen as a first step toward the creation of a European state. It was assumed that the Euro would create pressure to introduce this state.

The real reason the German government, traditionally opposed to the socialist vision, finally accepted the Euro, had to do with German reunification. The deal was as follows: France builds its European empire and Germany gets its reunification.[16] It was maintained that Germany would otherwise become too

---

[16] Until today, the French government has succeeded in building a disproportionate influence in the EU. Most EU institutions are hosted by France and Belgium and modelled on the French system of governance. French is a working language in the EU, next to English. But not German, even though the Union has far more German-speaking citizens. In the weighted influence of the member states based on their population, France is overrepresented and Germany is underrepresented. In fact, Germany's weighted influence did not increase at all after reunification. As Larsson ("National Policy in Disguise," p. 165) writes: "In short, the EU and its predecessors are primarily of French design, which, apart from official declarations, have in many respects served the purpose of using all possible means to enlarge, or at least maintain, French political world influence, particularly in Europe."

Bernard Connolly, who worked for the European Commission before being fired for writing his book [Bernard Connolly, *The Rotten Heart of Europe: The Dirty War for Europe's Money* (London: Faber and Faber, 1995), p. 4], supports this view: "The Commission staff engine has always been tuned to support French interests in particular." As Judt, *Postwar*, p. 308 states: "The EEC was a Franco-German condominium, in which Bonn underwrote the Community's finances and Paris dictated its politicies." In the same way Charles de Gaulle once said: "The EEC is a horse and a carriage: Germany is the horse and France is the coachman." (Quoted in Connolly, *The Rotten Heart of Europe*, p. 7.) Nothing seems to have changed up to this date.

powerful and its sharpest weapon, the Deutschmark, had to be taken away—in other words, disarmament.[17]

The next step in the plan of the socialist camp was the draft of a European constitution (by French ex-President Valery Giscard d'Estaing), establishing a central state. But the constitution project failed utterly; it was voted down by voters in France and the Netherlands in 2005. As is often the case, Germans had not even been asked. They had not been asked on the question of the Euro either. But politicians usually do not give up until they get what they want. In this case they just renamed the constitution; and it no longer required a popular vote in many countries.

As a consequence, the Lisbon Treaty was passed in December 2007. The Treaty is full of words like *pluralism, non-discrimination, tolerance* and *solidarity,* all of which can be interpreted as calls to infringe upon private property rights and the freedom of contract. In Article Three, the European Union pledges to fight social exclusion and discrimination, thereby opening the doors to interventionists. God is not mentioned once in the Lisbon Treaty.

In actuality, the Lisbon Treaty constitutes a defeat for the socialist ideal. It is not a genuine constitution but merely a treaty. It is a dead end for Empire advocates, who were forced to regroup and focus on the one tool that they had left—the Euro. But how, exactly, does it provoke a centralization in Europe?

The Euro causes the kinds of problems which can be viewed as a pretext for centralization on the part of politicians. Indeed, the construction and setup of the Euro have themselves provoked a chain of severe crises: member states are incentivized to use the printing press to finance their deficits; this feature of the EMU invariably leads to a sovereign debt crisis. The crisis, in turn, may be used to centralize power and fiscal policies. The centralization of fiscal policies may then be used to harmonize taxation and get rid of tax competition.

In the current sovereign debt crisis, the Euro, the only means left for the socialists to strengthen their case and achieve their

---

[17] More on the history of the Euro can be found in Chapter 9.

central state, is at stake. It is, therefore, far from the truth that the end of the Euro would mean the end of Europe or the European idea; it would be just the end of the socialist version of it.

Naturally one can have an economically integrated Europe with its four basic liberties without a single fiat currency. The UK, Sweden, Denmark, and the Czech Republic do not have the Euro, but belong to the common market enjoying the four liberties. If Greece were to join these countries, the classical liberal vision would remain untouched. In fact, a free choice of currency is more akin to the European value of liberty than a European legal tender coming along with a monopolistic money producer.

CHAPTER TWO

The Dynamics of Fiat Money

In order to understand the dynamics of the Euro, we have to delve into the history of money itself. Money, i.e., the common and generally accepted medium of exchange, emerged as a means to solve the problem of the double coincidence of wants. The problem of the double coincidence of wants consists in the problem of finding someone who owns what we want, and at the same time, wants what we have to offer. At some point in history some individuals discovered that they could satisfy their ends in a more efficient way: if they did not demand the goods that they needed directly, but rather goods that were more easily exchangeable. They used their production to demand a good that they would use as a medium of exchange; to buy, in an indirect way, what they really wanted.

A hunter, for instance, does not exchange his meat directly for the clothes he needs because it is difficult to find a cloth producer who needs meat right now and is willing to offer a good price. Rather, the hunter sells his production for wheat that is more marketable. Then, he uses the wheat to buy the clothes. In this way, wheat acquires an additional demand. It is not only demanded as a consumer good to eat or as a factor of production in farming, but also to be used as a medium of exchange. When the hunter is successful with his strategy, he may want to repeat it. Others may copy him. Thus, the demand for wheat as a medium of exchange rises and becomes more widespread. As the use of wheat as a medium of exchange becomes more widespread, it becomes ever more marketable and attractive to use it as such.

There may be other competing media of exchange at the same time. In a competitive process, one or a few media of exchange become generally accepted. They become money. In this competitive process, some commodities prove to be more useful to fulfil the function of a good medium of exchange and a store of value. Precious metals like gold and silver became money. In retrospect, it is not difficult to see why: gold and silver are homogeneous, resistant, of great value and strongly demanded, as well as easy to store and transport.

ENTER BANKS

When banks arose anew in the Renaissance in Northern Italy, gold and silver were still the dominant media of exchange. People used precious metals in their daily exchanges and when they deposited their money with banks, banks were paid for safekeeping and held one hundred percent reserves.[1]

Depositors would go to bankers and deposit a hundred grams of gold for safekeeping in a demand deposit contract. The depositor would then receive a certificate for his deposit which he could redeem at any time. Gradually these certificates started to circulate and were used in exchanges as if they were gold. The certificates were only rarely redeemed for physical gold. There was always a basic amount of gold lying around in the vault that was not demanded for redemption by clients. Consequently, the temptation for bankers to use some of the deposited gold for their own purposes was almost irresistible. Bankers often used the gold to grant loans to clients. They would start to issue fake certificates or create new deposits without having the gold

---

[1] Jesús Huerta de Soto, *Money, Bank Credit and Economic Cycles*, 2nd ed. (Auburn, Ala.: Ludwig von Mises Institute, [2006] 2009), describes the history of monetary deposit contracts. He shows that these contracts already existed in ancient times and that the obligations of these contracts were violated by bankers. Bankers used the money given to them as deposits for their own affairs. The story of misappropriation of deposited money repeats itself later in the Renaissance.

to back them up. In other words, bankers started to hold only fractional reserves.

ENTER THE STATE

Governments started to get heavily involved in banking. Unfortunately, interventions are a slippery slope, as Mises in his book, *Interventionism*,[2] has pointed out. Government interventions cause problems from the point of view of the interventionists themselves: begging for additional interventions to solve these additional problems, or the abolition of the initial intervention. If the course of adding new interventions is chosen, additional problems may arise that demand new interventions and so on. The road of interventions was taken in the field of money, finally leading to fiat money and the Euro. The Euro begs for a political centralization in Europe. The end result of monetary interventions is a world fiat currency.

The first intervention of governments into money was the monopolization of the mint; then came coin debasement. Governments would collect existing coins, melt them and reduce the content of precious metal in them, and cash in on the difference.

Profits made from the monopoly of the mint and reducing the quality of existing coins were considerable and turned the attention of government to the area of money. But coin debasement was a rather clumsy way of increasing government budgets. Banking had more potential, and provided a more sinister means of increasing government funds. Governments started to work together with bankers and become their accomplices. As a first favor to banks, governments did not enforce private legal norms for deposit contracts.

In a deposit contract, the obligation of the depository is to hold, at all times, a hundred percent of the deposited stuff or its equivalent in quantity and quality (*tantundem*). This implies that bankers have to hold one hundred percent reserves for all deposited money. Governments failed to enforce these laws

---

[2] Ludwig von Mises, *Interventionism: An Economic Analysis* (online edition: Ludwig von Mises Institute, 2004), http://mises.org.

for banks and to defend the property rights of depositors. Governments looked aside and ignored the problem. Finally, they even legalized the existing practice officially and allowed for ambiguous contracts. Effectively, banks got the privilege of holding fractional reserves and creating money. They could create "gold certificates" and deposits on their books even though they did not have the corresponding physical gold in their vaults.

Unbacked "gold certificates" and deposits are called *fiduciary media*. The privilege of producing fiduciary media was given to banks in exchange for strong cooperation with governments. In fact, governments looked away in the beginning when banks dishonored their safekeeping obligations because the newly created fiduciary media were given to governments in the form of loans. This cooperation between banks and governments continues until today and is illustrated in the forms of social and leisure contact of all sorts, support in times of crisis, and finally, in the form of bailouts.

THE CLASSICAL GOLD STANDARD

The gold standard reigned from 1815 to 1914. This was a period during which most countries turned to the single use of gold as money; it is easier to control one commodity money than two. Thus, governments followed market tendencies toward one generally accepted medium of exchange. The different currencies like the mark, pound or dollar, were just different terms for certain weights of gold. Exchange rates were "fixed." Everyone was using the same money, namely gold. Consequently, international trade and cooperation increased during this period.

The classical gold standard was, however, a fractional gold standard and, consequently, unstable. Banks did not hold one hundred percent reserves. Their deposits and notes were not backed one hundred percent by physical gold in their vaults. Banks were always confronted with the threat of losing reserves and being unable to redeem deposits. Due to this threat, the power of banks to create money was restricted. Creating money meant substantial profits, but bank runs and the risk of losing reserves limited banks in their credit expansion. Money users posed a constant threat to bank liquidity, as they would still use gold in their exchanges and demand redemption, especially when confidence in banks faded. Also, other banks that accumulated fiduciary media (notes issued by other banks) could present them for redemption at the issuing bank, threatening its reserve base. Thus, banks had an interest in changing the standard.

A fractional gold standard poses yet another threat to banks. When banks create new money and lend it to entrepreneurs, there is an artificial downwards pressure on interest rates. By artificially reducing interest rates and expanding credits, the correspondence of savings and investments is disturbed. Additional and longer investment projects may be successfully completed only when savings increase. When savings increase, interest rates tend to fall, indicating to entrepreneurs that it is possible to engage in new, formerly submarginal projects that were not profitable at higher interest rates. Now they may be successfully completed; after all, savings have increased and more resources are available for their completion.

When, however, banks expand credit and artificially reduce interest rates, entrepreneurs are likely to be deceived. With lower interest rates, more investment projects seem to be profitable—even though savings have not increased. At some point, price changes make it obvious that some of these newly started projects are unprofitable and must be liquidated due to a lack of resources.[3] More projects have been started than can be completed with the available resources. There are not enough savings. Interest rates fall due to credit expansion and not due to more savings. The purge of malinvestments is healthy; it realigns the structure of production and savings/consumption preferences.

---

[3] As the most comprehensive treaty on business cycle theory see Huerta de Soto, *Money, Bank Credit and Economic Cycles.*

During a recession, i.e., the widespread liquidation of malinvestments, banks normally get into trouble. Malinvestments and liquidations imply bad loans and losses for banks, threatening their solvency. As banks become less solvent, people start to lose confidence in them. Banks have a hard time finding creditors, depositors redeem their deposits, and bank runs are common. Consequently, banks become illiquid and often insolvent. Bankers became aware of these difficulties amid recessions, noting that difficulties were ultimately caused by their own creation of new money, and lending it at artificially low interest rates. They know that their business of fractional reserve banking has always been threatened by recurring recessions.

Bankers, however, do not want to forgo the profitable business of money production. Thus they demand government assistance (intervention). One great help for banks was and is the introduction of a central bank as a lender of last resort: central banks may lend to troubled banks to stem off panics. In a recession, troubled banks can receive loans from the central bank and thereby be saved.

Central banks provide banks with another advantage. They can supervise and control credit expansion. The danger of uncoordinated credit expansion is that more expansionary banks lose reserves to less expansionary banks. Redistribution of reserves is a danger if banks do not expand in the same tempo. If bank A expands faster than bank B, fiduciary media will find their way to bank B customers who present them at bank B for redemption. Bank B takes the fiduciary media and demands the gold from Bank A, which loses reserves.

If both banks expand at the same pace, however, customers will present the same amount of fiduciary media. Their mutual claims cancel each other out. The credit expansion lowers their reserve ratios, but banks do not lose gold (or base money) reserves to competitors. But without coordinated expansion there is the danger of reserve losses and illiquidity. In order to coordinate, they can form a cartel—but the danger always remains that one bank might leave the cartel, threatening the collapse of the others.

The solution to this problem is the introduction of a central bank that can coordinate credit expansion.

By coordinating credit expansion, credit can expand further because the danger of reserve losses to other banks disappears. In addition, the existence of a lender of last resort fosters credit expansion. In troubled times, a bank may always be able to get a loan from the central bank. This safety net makes banks extend more credits. As the potential for credit expansion grows, so does the potential for booms and malinvestments.

Even with the introduction of central banks, governments did not have total power over money. While the banking system could produce fiduciary media, money production was still connected to and restricted by gold. People could still go to banks in a recession and demand redemption in gold. Even though gold reserves were finally centralized in central banks, these reserves could prove to be insufficient to forestall a banking panic and a collapse of the banking system. Consequently, the ability to expand credit and to produce money in order to finance the government directly and indirectly (via bond purchases by the banking system) was still limited by the link to gold. Gold provided discipline. The temptation, naturally, for both banks and governments was to gradually remove all connection between money and gold.

A first experience of this removal of gold came at the start of World War I. Participating nations suspended redemption into specie, with the exception of the United States, who joined the war in 1917. War participants wanted to be able to inflate without limits in order to finance the war. As a consequence, there was a short episode of flexible exchange rates for fiat paper currencies. In the 1920s many nations returned to the gold standard, e.g., Great Britain in 1926 and Germany in 1924. However, redemption into gold was only possible at the central bank in form of bullion (the system is, therefore, called a *gold bullion standard*). The small bank customer was unable to get his gold back. Gold coins disappeared from circulation. Bullion, in turn, was only used for large international transactions. Great Britain redeemed pounds not only in gold, but also in dollars. Other countries redeemed their currencies in pounds. The centralization of reserves and the reduced redemption into cash allowed for a greater credit expansion, causing greater malinvestments and cycles.

THE SYSTEM OF BRETTON WOODS

Redemption was suspended in many countries during the Great Depression. The chaos of fluctuating exchange rates and competing devaluations prompted the United States to organize a new international monetary system in 1946. With the Bretton Woods System, central banks could redeem dollars into gold at the Federal Reserve. Private citizens were no longer able to redeem their money into gold, not even at the central bank. They were effectively robbed of their gold. The gold became property of the central bank. In such a *gold exchange standard*, only central banks and foreign governments can redeem currencies with other central banks.

Under the Bretton Woods system, each currency stood in a fixed relationship to the dollar, and thereby to gold. The dollar became the reserve currency for central banks. Central banks used their dollar reserves to inflate their currency on top. In this next step in the interventionist path in the monetary field, it became even easier to create money during recessions to help banks—but not private citizens.

The Bretton Woods system led to its own destruction, however. The United States had strong incentives to inflate its own currency and export it to other countries. The US produced dollars to buy goods and services and pay for wars in Korea and Vietnam. Goods flew into the US in exchange for dollars. European countries such as France, Western Germany, Switzerland, and Italy followed a less inflationary monetary policy under the influence of economists familiar with the Austrian school of economics. The gold reserve ratio of the Fed was reduced and overvalued dollars accumulated in European central banks until Charles de Gaulle finally initiated a run, presenting French dollars for gold at the Federal Reserve. In contrast to France, and due to Germany's military dependence on American troops, the Bundesbank agreed to hold on to the majority of its dollar reserves.[4] As American gold reserves dwindled, Nixon finally suspended redemption in August of 1971. Currencies started to float in 1973. Interventionist dynamics had pushed the world to irredeemable fiat currencies. With fiat paper currencies, there is no link to gold and thereby no limit to the production of paper money. Credit expansion can continue because doors are open for unlimited bailouts of either the government or the banking system.

EUROPE AFTER BRETTON WOODS

After the collapse of Bretton Woods, the world was dealing in fluctuating fiat currencies. Governments could finally control the money supply without any limitation to gold, and deficits could be financed by central banks. The manipulation of the quantity of money has only one aim: the financing of government policies. There is no other reason to manipulate the quantity of money.

Indeed, virtually any quantity of money is sufficient to fulfil money's function as a medium of exchange. If there is more money, prices are higher; and if there is less, money prices are lower. Imagine adding or subtracting zeros on fiat money notes. It would not disturb money's function as a medium of exchange. Yet, changes in the quantity of money have distributional effects. The first receivers of new money can buy at the old, still low prices. When the money enters the economy, prices are pushed up. Later receivers of the new money see prices increase before their incomes increase. There is redistribution in favor of the first receivers/producers of the new money to the detriment of the last receivers of the new money—who become continually poorer. The first receivers of the new money are mainly the banking system, the government, and connected industries, while later receivers are that part of the population having less intimate contact with the government, for example, fixed income groups.

---

[4] Germany continued to pay billions of dollars to keep American troops in the country as protection against potential Soviet invasion.

The new system of fiat currencies allowed almost unrestricted inflation of the money supply with huge redistribution effects. After the end of Bretton Woods, European banks inflated to finance expanding welfare states and subsidize companies. But not all countries inflated their currencies at the same pace. As a consequence, strong fluctuations in exchange rates negatively affected trade between European nations. As trade was negatively affected, the division of labor was also hampered, resulting in welfare losses. Politicians wanted to avert these losses; losses meant lower tax revenues. In addition, they feared that with a flight into real values, competitive devaluations and price inflation could get out of control. Companies and banks also dreaded this scenario. Moreover, fixed income receivers became upset when they saw their real income eroding. Savings rates decreased, reducing long term growth prospects.

Widely fluctuating exchange rates were the most important problem from the point of view of the political elite. European economic integration was in danger of falling apart. The four liberties of free movement of capital (foreign direct investments), goods, services, and people were in practice inhibited. Uncertainty caused by fluctuating exchange rates reduced movements severely. Moreover, fluctuating exchange rates were embarrassing for the faster inflating politicians and constituted a smoking gun. Politicians aimed, therefore, at a stabilization of exchange rates. But this was like putting a square peg in a round hole: fluctuating fiat currencies with diverging inflation rates cannot finance diverging government needs and provide stable exchange rates. Politicians wanted a way to coordinate inflation in the European Union that was similar to the ways of the fractional reserve banks, which must coordinate their expansion in order to maintain their reserve base.

The European Monetary System (EMS), which came about in 1979, was expected to be a solution for the coordination problem and an institutionalization of the former existing "snake."[5]

---

[5] Between 1972 and 1973 there was, for a short time, a system called "the snake in the tunnel." In this informal system currencies were allowed to fluctuate ±2.25 percent against each other. The tunnel was provided by the dollar. The

It was a legal formalization of the previous existing system of currencies that were supposed to fluctuate within small limits. Politicians and big businesses interested in foreign trade had worked on it together as an attempt to control diverging inflation rates. France, Germany, Italy, Belgium, the Netherlands, Luxembourg, Denmark and Ireland all participated in this attempt to stabilize their exchange rates. Spain joined it after it entered the European Union in 1986. The system, however, was a misconstruction. There was no redemption into gold or any other commodity money. The EMS was built on paper.[6]

The EMS was also an attempt to restrain the hegemony of the Bundesbank with a relatively less inflationary monetary policy, and prevent it from stepping out of the line. The Banque de France is known to have internally discussed the "tyranny of the mark."[7] The French government had even wanted the EMS to include a pooling of central bank reserves, thereby obtaining access to German reserves. But this request was declined by Bundesbankers who were very sceptical about the whole project. After its creation, German chancellor Helmut Schmidt threatened

---

Smithsonian agreements had set ±2.25 percent bands for currencies to move relative to the US dollar. When the dollar started to fluctuate freely in 1973, the tunnel disappeared. The snake left the tunnel and a Deutschmark-dominated block remained, with currencies fluctuating ± 2.25 percent. As the Bundesbank was no longer obliged to buy the excess supply of dollars, it could raise interest rates and restrict liquidity. While the French government wanted to influence the economy by credit expansion, the German institutions wanted to fight against inflation. France left the snake in 1974. It returned in 1975 in an attempt to reduce German hegemony, but was gone again one year later. In 1977, only Germany, Benelux and Denmark remained in a de facto Mark zone. For more on the history of the snake and the EMU, see Ivo Maes, J. Smets and J. Michielsen, "EMU from a Historical Perspective," in Maes, Ivo, *Economic Thought and the Making of European Monetary Union, Selected Essays by Ivo Maes* (Cheltenham, UK: Edgar Elgar, 2004), pp. 131–191.

[6] On the failings of the EMS see Murray Rothbard, "Schöne neue Zeichengeldwelt," in *Das Schein-Geld-System: Wie der Staat unser Geld zerstört,* trans. Guido Hülsmann (Gräfelfing: Resch, 2000).

[7] See David Marsh, *Der Euro – Die geheime Geschichte der neuen Weltwährung,* trans. Friedrich Griese (Hamburg: Murmann, 2009), p. 21. Maes, Smets, and Michielsen ("EMU from a Historical Perspective," p. 171) write that French politicians understood, "that only a European pooling of national monetary policies could put an end to German dominance."

to draft a law ending the bank's formal independence if the Bundesbankers would not agree to the EMS.

The EMS tried to fix exchange rates that had been allowed to float in a corridor of ±2.25 percent around the official rate. But the intention of fixed exchange rates was incompatible with the system built to achieve that aim. The idea was that when the exchange rate would threaten to leave the corridor, central banks would intervene to bring the rate back into the corridor. For this to happen, a central bank would have to sell its currency, or in other words, produce more money when the currency was appreciating and moving above the corridor. It would have to buy its currency, selling assets such as foreign exchange reserves, if its currency was depreciating, falling below the corridor.

The Spanish Central Bank provides us with a good example. If the peseta appreciated too much in relation to the Deutschmark, the Bank of Spain had to inflate and produce pesetas to bring the peseta's price down. The central bank was probably very happy to do so. As it could produce pesetas without limits, nothing could stop the Bank of Spain from preventing an appreciation of the peseta. However, if the peseta depreciated against the Deutschmark, the Bank of Spain would have to buy its currency and sell its Deutschmark reserves or other assets, thereby propping up the exchange rate. This could not be done without limits, but was strictly limited to the reserves of the Bank of Spain. This was the basic misconstruction of the EMS and the reason it could not work. It was not possible to force another central bank to cooperate, i.e., to force the Bundesbank to buy peseta with newly produced Deutschmarks when the peseta was depreciating. In fact, the absence of such an obligation was a result of the resistance of the Bundesbank. France called for a course of required action that would reduce the independence of the Bundesbank. Bundesbank president Otmar Emminger resisted being obliged to intervene on part of falling currencies in the EMS. He finally got his way and the permission from Helmut Schmidt to suspend interventions leading to the purchase of foreign currencies within the EMS agreements.[8] Countries with falling currencies had to support their currencies themselves.

Indeed, an obligation to intervene in favor of falling currencies would have created perverse incentives. A central bank that inflated rapidly would have forced others to follow. Fiat paper currencies are introduced for redistribution within a country. Fixed fiat exchange rates coupled with an obligation to intervene allowed for redistribution between countries. In such a setup, the faster inflating central bank (Bank of Spain) would force another central bank (Bundesbank) to follow and buy up faster, inflating one's currency. The Bank of Spain could produce pesetas that would be exchanged into Deutschmarks buying German goods. Later the Bundesbank would have to produce Deutschmarks to buy peseta and stabilize the exchange rate. There would be a redistribution from the slower-inflating central bank to the faster-inflating central bank.

Yet, in the EMS there was no obligation to buy the faster-inflating currency. This implied also that the EMS could not fulfil its purpose of guaranteeing stable exchange rates. Fixed fiat exchange rates are impossible to guarantee when participating central banks are independent. Governments wanted both fiat money production for redistributive internal reasons and stable exchange rates. This desire makes voluntary cooperation in the pace of inflation necessary. Without voluntary cooperation, coordinated inflation is impossible. The Bundesbank was usually the spoilsport of coordinated inflation. It did not inflate fast enough when other central banks, such as the Bank of Italy, inflated the money supply to finance Italian public deficits.

The Bundesbank did not inflate as much on account of German monetary history. A single generation had lost almost all monetary savings two times, namely, after two world wars: in the hyperinflation of 1923 and the currency reform in 1948. Most Germans wanted hard money, and expressed that through the institutional set up of the Bundesbank, which was relatively independent of the government. What all of this means is that, in practice, the EMS would only function if central banks were

---

[8] See Marsh, *Der Euro*, pp. 135–136.

only able to inflate as much as the slowest links in the chain: the Bundesbank and its traditional ally, De Nederlandsche Bank.

Central banks produce money primarily to finance government deficits. Consequently, governments can only have deficits not larger than those of the soundest link in the chain—often the German government. The Bundesbank was the brakeman of European inflation: a hated corrective. It was widely regarded as uncooperative because it did not want to produce money as fast as other central banks. It forced other central banks controlled by their governments to stop when they wanted to continue, or forced embarrassing readjustments of the corridor through its stubbornness.[9]

In fact, there were several readjustments of the exchange rates in the EMS.[10] The final crisis of the EMS occurred in 1992 when the Spanish peseta and the Irish pound had to readjust their exchange rates. The British pound came under pressure in the same year. After a critical interview on the pound given by the President of the Bundesbank, Helmut Schlesinger, the British government had to stop trying to stabilize the exchange rate and left the EMS. Famously, George Soros contributed to speeding up the collapse. The French Franc soon came under pressure as well. France wanted unlimited and unconditional support by the

---

[9] The best work describing the struggle of European governments wanting higher spending on one side and the Bundesbank trying to maintain inflation limited on the other side is Bernard Connolly's *The Rotten Heart of Europe*. Connolly shows the dominance of the Bundesbank in many instances. The dominance of the Bundesbank is also illustrated by an anecdote recalled by Rüdiger Dornbusch, as told in Joachim Starbatty, "Anmerkungen zum Woher und Wohin der Europäischen Union," *Tübinger Diskussionsbeitrag* no. 292 (2005), p. 13. At a dinner, the then President of the De Nederlandsche Bank, Wim Duisenberg, was passed a note. He passed it on to his vice president, who also read it. Both nodded and gave the note back. When Dornbusch asked what was written on the note, he was told that the Bundesbank had raised its rates 50 basis points. The nodding meant that they would follow and also raise 50 basis points.

[10] Within the very first years—from spring of 1979 to the spring of 1983—there were seven readjustments alone. The readjustments implied an average appreciation of twenty-seven percent of the Deutschmark. In total, there were twenty two readjustments over the whole period of the EMS from 1979 to 1997.

Bundesbank in favor of the franc.[11] Yet the Bundesbank was not willing to buy francs without limits.

Not surprisingly, governments and central banks wanted to escape the "tyranny" of the Bundesbank. The system finally failed. The declaration of surrender was made when the corridor was amplified to ± 15 percent in 1993. The Bundesbank had won; it had forced the others to declare the bankruptcy. It had followed its hard money philosophy and not succumbed to the pressure of other governments. Anyone who inflated more than the Bundesbank was showing its citizens a weak currency. The Deutschmark, in turn, was respected throughout the world and very popular among Germans. It brought relative monetary stability not only to Germany, but to the rest of Europe as well. The Deutschmark, of course, only looked stable in comparison to the rest. It itself was highly inflationary and lost nine tenths of its purchasing power from its birth in 1948 to the end of the EMS.

The success of the Bundesbank's resisting inflationary pressures, unfortunately, was a pyrrhic victory. The EMS had had important psychological effects. Europeans, including Germans, believed that there was a European "system" that had stabilized exchange rates somewhat. But it was an illusion. There had been no "system," just independent central banks inflating at different rates and trying to stabilize their own rates to some degree. This illusion reduced the distrust of central European institutions. The public was now psychologically prepared for a European currency. Government propaganda presented it as the logical next step in a "European Monetary System."

The single European currency was the final solution for European governments with inflationary desires: one could get rid of the brakes that the Bundesbank was putting on deficit financing of European states and enjoy a stable exchange rate at the same time. The solution meant the factual abolition of the spirit and power of the Bundesbank. If Europeans had just wanted monetary stability and a single currency in Europe,

---

[11] Marsh, *Der Euro*, p. 241. In the early 1980s in a similar situation the French government had threatened to leave the EMS and impose import duties if the Bundesbank would not support the franc.

Europe could just have introduced the Deutschmark in all other countries. But nationalism would not allow for this. With a single currency, there were no embarrassing exchange rate movements that would reveal a central bank's inflating faster than its neighbors. For the first time there was a centralized money producer in Europe that could help to finance government debts, and open new dimensions for government interventions, and redistribution of wealth.

CHAPTER THREE

The Road Toward the Euro

The Werner plan had been the first attempt to establish a common fiat currency in Europe. It was drawn up by a group surrounding Pierre Werner, Prime Minister of Luxembourg, and presented in October of 1970. The plan entailed three stages and called for a monetary union by 1980. In stage one, budgetary policies were coordinated and exchange rate fluctuations were reduced. The third stage fixed exchange rates and converged economic policies. But it was not clear how to get from the first to the third stage; stage two had never been spelt out. The Werner plan did not call for a common central bank, and it was finally dropped after France left the snake in 1974. Nevertheless, it set a first precedent toward European integration, a supposedly essential goal.

The plan for a common currency was revived by Jacques Delors, a president of the European Commission for ten years and an individual with a long career in French socialist politics.[1] A technocrat and a politician through and through, he was raised in the spirit of French interventionism and pushed

---

[1] As Connolly, *The Rotten Heart of Europe*, p. 75 writes: "Delors is a French nationalist as well as a Euronationalist. How is this contradiction resolved? He sees the creation of 'Europe' as the best way of extending French influence. In his ten years in Brussels he assiduously packed the Commission with French Socialists: the Commission became, to a large extent, a French Socialist machine. His hope, rather clearly, was that 'Europe' would be run by the Commission and thus dominated by France." See also pp. 104, 380.

toward political integration and harmonization during his terms as president of the Commission. The Single European Act of 1986 (one year after Delors took over the European Commission) was a step toward political union. It was the first major revision of the Treaty of Rome and its objective was the establishment of the Single Market by December 31, 1992. One of its long term goals was a single currency, and majority voting (in contrast to the previously prevailing unanimity voting) was introduced into new areas such as currency, social policy, economics, scientific research and environmental policies.

In 1987, pressure toward a single currency intensified. Helmut Schmidt, a social democratic and former chancellor of Germany, and Valery Giscard d'Estaing, a former president of France, founded the lobbying group "Association for the monetary union of Europe." Large German companies such as Volkswagen, Daimler-Benz, Commerzbank, Deutsche Bank and Dresdner Bank soon became members.

In April 1989, the Delors Report, a three stage plan for the introduction of the Euro, was published. It was a milestone on the road toward the Euro. At the summit of Rome in December 1990, i.e., two months after the German reunification, the three-stage plan was officially adopted, based on the long-term goals as established in the Single European Act.

The first stage had been underway since July of 1990 with strengthened economic and monetary coordination. Exchange rate controls were eliminated and the common market was completed.

In January 1990, Helmut Kohl agreed with Mitterrand to approve the single currency according to Kohl's foreign adviser, Joachim Bitterlich.[2] But Bundesbankers still saw the single currency as an undesirable end for the then-near future.

Karl Otto Pöhl, President of the Bundesbank at the time, was confident that the single currency could be prevented. For Pöhl the monetary union was a bizarre idea. He argued that a monetary union would only be possible given a future political union—which was still far off. His tactic was to define conditions

---

[2] Bandulet, *Die letzten Jahre des Euro,* p. 52.

for a currency union that France and other states would never accept.[3] But he miscalculated. The French government accepted a central bank based on the model of the Bundesbank, and Kohl had to give up his aim of introducing monetary and political union in a parallel way.

The political will favoring a uniform currency was expressed in the Maastricht Treaty, signed on December 9 and 10, 1991. In Maastricht, Kohl distanced himself from the aim of a political union, but went ahead and sacrificed the Mark. He also agreed to set a date for the introduction of the single currency: January 1, 1999. Moreover, participation in the monetary union was not voluntary for countries who signed the Treaty. This implied that Germany could be forced to participate in the monetary union in 1999.

The Treaty set down the details of the introduction of the Euro and also the start date for the second stage of the Delors Report: 1994. In the second stage, from 1994 to 1998, the European Monetary Institute, the forerunner of the ECB, was founded, and participants in the monetary union would be elected. Five criteria for selection were negotiated and established.

1. Price inflation rates had to be under a limit set by the average of the three aspirants, with the lowest inflation rates + 1.5 percent.

2. Public deficits had to be not higher than three percent of GDP.

3. Total public debts had to be not over sixty percent of GDP.

4. Long term interest rates had to be under a limit established by the average of the three governments paying the lowest interest rates + two percent.

5. Countries had to join the European Monetary System for at least two years and could not devalue its currency during this period.

---

[3] Bandulet, *Die letzten Jahre des Euro*, p. 53.

The fulfilment of these criteria was facilitated by the political will demonstrated in favor of the Euro. The support in a common monetary system implied that interest rates converged. As expectations for an entry in the Eurozone increased, highly indebted governments had to pay lower interest rates. Also, inflation rates decreased in highly inflationary countries as people expected a lower inflation of the Euro than they did of the preceding currencies.

The German government tried to impose automatic sanctions in the case of any infringement of the deficit limit after the Euro had been introduced. But Theodor Waigel, the German Minister of Finance, did not succeed. In talks in Dublin in December of 1996, other governments rejected automatic sanctions on countries with deficit overruns. On January 1, 1997, the legal framework of the Euro and the European Central Bank was established. The participants and the monetary instruments of the ECB were determined in the beginning of 1998.

Finally, the third stage of the Delors Report commenced with the official introduction of the Euro on January 1, 1999. Exchange rates between the participating currencies were permanently fixed. The third stage was completed when, three years later, the Euro was introduced into circulation.

GERMANY'S COUP D'ÉTAT

The introduction of the Euro in Germany resembled a coup d'état.[4] The Bundesbank had supported a British 1989 proposal by Nigel Lawson concerning currency competition in the European Community including the new currency ECU (European Currency Unit). There would be thirteen currencies in the EU, with all thirteen accepted as legal tender. A year later John Major made another attempt for Britain when he proposed the ECU to be made a hard currency which could be issued by a European central bank coexisting with the national currencies.

---

[4] Roland Baader, *Die Euro-Katastrophe. Für Europas Vielfalt – gegen Brüssels Einfalt* (Böblingen: Anita Tykve, 1993).

But the German government rejected the British free market proposal. It preferred the socialist proposal of one fiat money for Europe. The German government acted against the will of the majority of Germans who wanted to keep the Deutschmark. The government launched an advertising campaign, putting ads in newspapers stating that the Euro would be as stable as the Deutschmark. The ad campaign's budget was raised from 5.5 to 17 million Deutschmarks when the Danes voted against the introduction of the Euro.

German politicians tried to convince their constituency with an absurd argument: they claimed that the Euro was necessary for maintaining peace in Europe. Former president Richard von Weizsäcker wrote that a political union implied an established monetary union, and that it would be necessary to maintain peace, seeing as Germany's central position in Europe had led to two World Wars.[5] Social democrat Günther Verheugen, in an outburst of arrogance and paternalism typical of the political class, claimed in a speech before the German parliament: "A strong, united Germany can easily—as history teaches—become a danger for itself and others."[6] Both men had forgotten that after the unification, Germany was not as big as it had been before World War II. Moreover, they did not acknowledge that the situation was quite different in other ways. Militarily, Germany was vastly inferior to France and Great Britain and was still occupied by foreign troops. And after the war, the allies had reeducated the Germans in the direction of socialism, progressivism and pacifism—to ward off any military opposition.[7]

---

[5] Weizsäcker, Richard von, "Meilenstein Maastricht," in *Frankfurter Allgemeine Zeitung*, April 13, 1992.

[6] This argument prevails until the present day, serving to justify the bailout of Greece. Wolfgang Schäuble stated on July 8, 2010: "We are the country in the middle of Europe. Germany has always been at the centre of every major war in Europe, but our interest is not to be isolated." See Angela Cullen and Rainer Buergin, "Schäuble Denied Twice by Merkel Defies Doctors in Saving Euro," *Bloomberg* (July 21, 2010), http://noir.bloomberg.com. He seems to imply that Germany had to bail out Greece in order to prevent another European war.

[7] On the reeducation of Germans see Caspar von Schrenk-Notzing, *Charakterwäsche. Die Re-education der Deutschen und ihre bleibenden Auswirkungen*, 2nd ed. (Graz: Ares Verlag, 2005).

The implicit blaming of Germany for World War II and making gains as a result was a tactic that the political class had often used. Now the implicit argument was that because of World War II and because of Auschwitz in particular, Germany had to give up the Deutschmark as a step toward political union. Here were paternalism and a culture of guilt at their best.[8]

In fact, German chancellor Helmut Schmidt, when speaking of the European Monetary System, the predecessor to the Euro, said that it was part of a strategy to spare Germany from fateful isolation in the heart of Europe. In 1978 he told Bundesbankers that Germany needed protection from the West due to its borders with communist countries. He added that Germany, in the aftermath of Auschwitz, was still vulnerable.[9] Germany needed to be integrated into NATO and into the European Community, and that the European Monetary System was a means to this end—as the Euro would be later. Upon re-reading his words in 2007, Schmidt stated that he had not changed his mind. He believed that without a unified currency, Germany's financial institutions would become leaders, causing envy and anger on the part of its neighbors, and bringing about adverse political consequences for Germany.

A similar threat of political isolation occurred later within the context of German reunification. Mitterrand had raised the possibility of a triple alliance between Great Britain, France and the Soviet Union, as well as an encirclement of Germany. Only the single currency would prevent such a scenario.[10]

While the German political class tried to convince sceptical Germans of the benefits of the single currency, German academics tried to persuade the political class of the single

---

[8] On the systematic use of guilt charges by foreign and national political elites in order to manipulate the German population toward these elites'goals see Heinz Nawratil, *Der Kult mit der Schuld. Geschichte im Unterbewußtsein* (München: Universitat, 2008). In a similar way, Hans-Olaf Henkel argues that the guilt complexes and fears stemming from Nazi times make German politicians timid still today and inhibit them from representing the interests of Germans. See Hans-Olaf Henkel, *Rettung unser Geld! Deutschland wird ausverkauft – Wie der Euro-Betrug unseren Wohlstand gefährdet* (München: Heyne, 2010), p. 30.

[9] Quoted in Marsh, *Der Euro*, pp. 68–69.

[10] See Marsh, *Der Euro*, p. 203.

currency's dangers and urged the government not to sign the Maastricht Treaty. Sixty economists signed a manifesto in 1992 claiming, among other things, that its provisions were too soft.[11] In 1998, 155 German economic professors demanded a delay of the monetary union (but to no avail). Structures of European countries would be too different to make it viable.[12] Even many Bundesbankers opposed the introduction of the Euro before a political union was achieved. They argued that a common currency should be an end but not the means of economic convergence. By stating that a political union would be a necessary requirement for a monetary union Bundesbankers hoped that the French government would stop pushing for the single currency. In an expression of disapproval the Bundesbank raised interest rates immediately after the drafting of the Maastricht Treaty in December 1991.[13]

Legal experts raised constitutional concerns about the Maastricht Treaty.[14] Law professor Karl Albrecht Schacht-schneider argued that a monetary union could only be stable and work in a political union. A political union, however,

---

[11] The German magazine *Der Focus* reported in 1997 that the EU Commission contracted 170 economists in all European countries. The economists had to convince the population of the Euro's advantages. See Günter Hannich, *Die kommende Euro-Katastrophe. Ein Finanzsystem vor dem Bankrott?* (München: Finanzbuch Verlag, 2010), p. 27.

[12] For an overview and discussion of the arguments brought forwards by these economists, see Renate Ohr, "The Euro in its Fifth Year: Expectations Fulfilled?" in *The Price of the Euro*, ed. Jonas Ljundberg (New York: Palgrave MacMillan, 2004), pp. 59–70, and Joachim Starbatty, "Sieben Jahre Währungsunion: Erwartungen und Realität," *Tübinger Diskussionsbeitrag* no. 208 (February 2006). Also academics in the U.S. brought forwards arguments against the EMU and interpreted the decision as political. See Barry Eichengreen, "Is Europe an Optimum Currency Area?" *NBER working paper series* no. 3579 (January 1991) and Martin Feldstein, "The Political Economy of the European Political and Monetary Union: Political Sources of an Economic Liability," *Journal of Economic Perspectives* 11 (24, 1997): pp. 23–42. For an overview of the opinion of U.S. economists see Lars Jonung and Eoin Drea, "It Can't Happen, It's a Bad Idea, It Won't Last: U.S. Economists on the EMU and the Euro, 1989–2002," *Econ Journal Watch* 7 (1, 2010): pp. 4–52.

[13] See Connolly, *The Rotten Heart of Europe*, pp. 74 and 302.

[14] German University professors Karl Albrecht Schachtschneider, Wilhelm Hank, Wilhelm Nölling and Joachim Starbatty filed a suit at the constitutional court against the introduction of the Euro.

implied the end of the German state, which itself was uncon-
stitutional. Schachtschneider also pointed out that the German
constitution demanded a stable currency, an end not achievable
in a monetary union with independent states. The right to property would also be violated in an inflationary monetary union.

The German constitutional court, however, found that the
Maastricht Treaty was in fact constitutional. The court stipulated that Germany could only participate in a stable currency,
and would have to leave the monetary union if it proved to be
unstable.

Finally, politicians changed the German constitution in order
to make the transfer of the sovereign power over the currency to
a supranational institution possible. All of this was done without
asking the people.

Furthermore, German politicians argued that the Euro would
be stable due to the convergence criteria, independence of the
ECB, and the sanctions that were institutionalized in the Stability and Growth Pact proposed by German Finance Minister,
Theo Waigel, in 1995.[15] But all three arguments ultimately failed.

The convergence criteria were not automatically and rou-
tinely applied, and the Council of the European Union could
still decide, with a qualitative majority, to admit countries to the
Eurozone. In fact, the Council finally admitted countries such as
Belgium and Italy, even though they did not fulfil the criterion
of the sixty percent limit of public debt to GDP. Even Germany
did not fulfil the criteria. Moreover, many countries only
fulfiled some criteria due to accounting tricks which postponed
expenditures into the future or generated one time revenues.
[16] Several countries managed to fulfil the criteria for 1997 only,

---

[15] The Stability and Growth Pact sets fiscal limits to member states in the Eurozone.

[16] Accounting tricks included manoeuvres with France Telecom, the Eurotax
in Italy, Treuhand in Germany, Germany's hospital debt, and an attempt to
revaluate gold reserves in several countries. See James D. Savage, *Making the
EMU. The Politics of Budgetary Surveillance and the Enforcement of Maastricht*
(Oxford: Oxford University Press, 2005).

the year during which the future members of the monetary union were appointed. Moreover, many countries only fulfiled the criteria because it was expected that they would join the monetary union. Thus, their interest rates fell, reducing the debt burden of public debts and deficits.

The Stability and Growth Pact (SGP) was not as harsh as Theo Waigel had suggested. When the SGP was finally signed in 1997, it had lost most of its disciplinary power. The result prompted Anatole Kaletsky to comment in *The Times* that the outcome of the Treaty of Maastricht represented the third capitulation of Germany to France within the century, citing as well the Treaty of Versailles and Potsdam Agreement.[17]

Waigel had wanted stricter limits than those set by Maastricht. He had wanted to restrict public deficits to one percent, and demanded automatic monetary sanction for violations of the limit. Revenues from fines would be distributed among members. Yet, after the French government had opposed the measure, sanctions did not become automatic, but dependent on political decisions, and it was decided that revenues would go to the EU.

The Commission of the EU was responsible for monitoring the SGP.[18] But even in the Commission there was no strong backing of the SGP. The Chairman of the European Commission, Romano Prodi, described its provisions as "stupid." In the case of eventual infringements of the provisions of the pact, the SGP establishes that the Commission is to give recommendations to the Council for Economic and Financial Affairs (EcoFin). EcoFin is comprised of the Economics and Finance Ministers of the EU and must meet once a month. U-pon the recommendation of the Commission, EcoFin decides, with a qualitative majority, if the criteria of the SGP are being fulfiled or not, and is then to issue warnings or announce the existence of excessive deficits. EcoFin offers recommendations to reduce the deficits. If the infringing government does not follow the recommendations and continues to miss the criteria, a majority of two thirds is

---

[17] Bandulet, *Die letzten Jahre des Euro*, p. 84.

[18] See Roy H. Ginsberg, *Demystifying the European Union. The Enduring Logic of Regional Integration* (Plymouth, UK: Rowman & Littlefield, 2007), p. 249.

necessary to establish sanctions. Fines can amount to a half percent of GDP.

Sinners were to decide for themselves if they would be punished. If several countries failed to fulfil the criteria, they could easily support each other and block sanctions. To date, no country has had to pay for its failure in this regard.

In November 2003, EcoFin waived sanctions recommended by the Commission against France and Germany. This triggered a discussion concerning the efficacy of the SGP. The already watered-down SGP met its end on the twentieth of March, 2005. Germany violated the three percent limit on public deficits for the third time in a row in 2005. As a consequence, EcoFin watered down the SGP even more by defining several situations and expenditures that would justify a violation of the three percent limit: natural catastrophes, a falling GDP, recessions, expenditures for innovation and research, public investments, expenditures for international solidarity and European politics, and pension reforms.[19]

The reform meant a carte blanche for deficits. Because politicians themselves decide if the sanctions of the SGP are applied, deficit countries never have to pay. Politicians later justify their behavior by watering down the SGP and effectively ending it.

The independence of the ECB is also questionable. No cen-tral bank is totally independent. Central bankers are nominated by politicians and their constitutions are subject to changes made by the parliament.

Politicians were quite frank about the "independence" of the ECB. François Mitterrand claimed that the ECB would execute the economic decisions of the Council of the European Union. In the conception of French politicians, the Council of the European Union controls the ECB. Fernand Herman, a Belgian member of the European Parliament, demanded that the central bank pursues the ends set by the Council and the Parliament, simultaneously guaranteeing price stability.[20]

---

[19] Bandulet, *Die letzten Jahre des Euro,* p. 97.

[20] Baader, *Die Euro-Katastrophe,* p. 195.

The Maastricht Treaty also establishes that exchange rate strategies are to be determined by politicians and not the ECB. The French government had even demanded (unsuccessfully) that politicians decide on short term exchange rate policies. Still, a political decision that the Euro exchange rate is overvalued and should depreciate stands in contrast with an autonomous operating of a stability guaranteeing central bank. It undermines the autonomy of the ECB.

DIFFERENCES BETWEEN THE BUNDESBANK AND THE ECB

Despite the assurances of German politicians that the ECB would be a copy of the Bundesbank, therefore exporting Bundesbank stability to the rest of Europe, and the ECB's symbolic location in Frankfurt, the two remain quite different.

From the beginning there were doubts about the independence of the ECB. Its first president, Wim Duisenberg, "voluntarily" stepped down halfway through his term in order to pass the presidency on to his French successor, Jean-Claude Trichet. Before the introduction of the Euro, Trichet, an engineer by training and a statist by mentality had strongly opposed the "independence" of the ECB. From the French government's point of view, the formal "independence" of the ECB was only the means necessary to get the German government to agree to a monetary union.[21] If necessary, the ECB could be put into the service of politics. In fact, this was the intention of French politicians. Mitterrand announced, before France's Maastricht referendum, that European monetary policy would not be dictated by the ECB. France imagined the ECB would ultimately be dependent on orders from the political sphere.[22]

---

[21] See Marsh, *Der Euro*, p. 287.

[22] Thus, Feldstein, "The Political Economy," p. 38, states: "France recognizes that the institution of the EMU will evolve over time and continually presses for some political body (an 'economic government') to exert control over ECB. It has already made significant progress toward that end." Mitterrrand said literally: "One hears it said that the European Central Bank will be the master of the decisions. It's not true! Economic policy belongs to the European Council and the application of monetary policy is the task of the [European]

An important difference is the accountability of the two institutions. The Bundesbank managed German monetary policy directly. As the German population is very adverse to inflation it was political suicide for politicians to attempt to influence the Bundesbank toward more inflation or to threaten its independence. Higher price inflation would mean that voters punished politicians and withdrew their support for the Bundesbank. It was on the support of the German population that the power of Bundesbankers vis-à-vis politicians was founded. In contrast, if there is price inflation in the Eurozone, both Bundesbankers and German politicians could say that they opposed inflationary monetary measures but that they were just outvoted by their European colleagues. They can blame others for rising prices. And Germans cannot vote the EU Commission out of office since it is not elected by the public.[23]

The difference between the two institutions can be seen in their official functions. The *Bundesbankgesetz* (Constitution of the Bundesbank, 1957) establishes guaranteeing the security of the currency as the main task of the Bundesbank (*Währungssicherheit*), i.e., price stability. The task of the ECB is more ambitious. The Treaty of Maastricht states that its primary objective "shall be to maintain price stability." Yet, "without prejudice of the objective of price stability, the [Eurosystem] shall support the general economic policies in the Community."[24] This addition is the result of pressure from the French government, which had always wanted direct political control over the printing press. This means that if official price inflation rates are low, the ECB can and actually must print money in order to support economic

---

Central Bank, in the framework of the decisions of the European Council . . . The people who decide economic policy, of which monetary policy is no more than a means of implementation, are the politicians." Quoted in Connolly, *The Rotten Heart of Europe*, p. 142. See also p. 248.

[23] See Stefan Homburg, "Hat die Währungsunion Auswirkungen auf die Finanzpolitik?," in Franz-Ulrich Willeke, ed., *Die Zukunft der D-Mark. Eine Streitschrift zur Europäischen Währungsunion* (München: Olzog, 1997), pp. 93–108.

[24] See Tommaso Padoa-Schioppa, *The Euro and its Central Bank* (Cambridge: MIT Press, 2004), for more details on the functions and strategies of the ECB.

policies. If price inflation is low and there is unemployment, the ECB must ease its policy stand.

Curiously, the ECB interprets price stability to mean rising prices. Before 2003, the ECB had a target for price inflation in a band of zero to two percent. Due to the widespread fear of deflation, central bankers want a buffer to zero.[25] In May of 2003, the ECB showed its tendency toward inflation by raising its target to just below two percent. At the same time, the ECB reduced the importance of its monetary growth pillar. The control of monetary growth quit being an intermediate end and became an indicator for the bank's policies.

The Bundesbank's legacy was further reduced in 2006 when the direction of the research department of the ECB passed from Otmar Issing, a German conservative, to Loukas Papademous, a Greek socialist who believes that price inflation is not a monetary phenomenon, but one caused by low unemployment.[26] In spring 2011 the dismantlement of the Bundesbank remains continued with the demission of Axel Weber. Weber had repeatedly criticized the inflationary policy of the ECB confronting a superiority of inflationary interests under an alliance of Latin countries lead by France. When it became apparent that he would not be able to push through his Bundesbank philosophy he stepped down as President of the Bundesbank and withdraw as the frontrunner from the race for the next President of the ECB. The influence of the Bundesbank was further pushed back.

The most important difference between the banks is that the ECB has a two pillar model while the Bundesbank had only one pillar: the Bundesbank focused on the evolution of monetary aggregates, i.e., inflation of the money supply. A deviation from its inflationary goals, as expressed by monetary aggregates, would always be corrected.

---

[25] On the irrational fear of deflation and the erroneous arguments brought forwards against it, see Philipp Bagus, "Deflation: When Austrians Become Interventionists," *Quarterly Journal of Austrian Economics* 6 (4, 2003): pp. 19–35, and "Five Common Errors about Deflation," *Procesos de Mercado: Revista Europea de Economía Política* 3 (1, 2006): pp. 105–123.

[26] See Roland Vaubel, "The Euro and the German Veto," *Econ Journal Watch* 7 (1, 2010): p. 87.

The ECB has a second pillar. It also relies on the analysis of economic indicators in its monetary policy decisions. The economic indicators include the evolution of wage rates, long term interest rates, exchange rates, price indexes, business and consumer confidence polls, output measures, and fiscal developments, etc. The ECB therefore has more discretionary power than the Bundesbank and can use the monetary press for economic stabilization. Even if money aggregates grow faster than intended, the ECB can argue that economic indicators allow for an expansionary policy. It has plenty of indicators to choose from as justification.

Another reason the ECB may not go for low inflation is that no central banker wants to pass into the history books as a trigger of a recession. A recession in Southern Europe puts immense pressure on the ECB to lower interest rates even though that might endanger monetary stability.

CHAPTER FOUR

Why High Inflation Countries Wanted the Euro

RIDDING EUROPE OF THE DEUTSCHMARK

Governments of Latin countries, and especially France, re-garded the Euro as an efficient means of getting rid of the hated Deutschmark.[1] Before the introduction of the Euro, the Deutschmark was a standard that laid bare the monetary mismanagement of irresponsible governments. While the Bundesbank inflated the money supply, it produced new money at a slower rate than the high inflation of—especially Southern European—countries, who used their central banks most generously to finance deficits. The exchange rate against the Deutschmark served citizens in those countries as a standard of comparison. Governments of high inflation countries feared the comparison with the Bundesbank. The Euro was a means to end the embarrassing comparisons and devaluations.

Governments of high inflation countries did not fear the newly established European Central Bank. While the new central bank would look like a copy of the Bundesbank from the outside, from the inside it could be put under political pressure

---

[1] As Connolly, *The Rotten Heart of Europe*, p. 4 states in 1995: "For the French élite, money is not the lubricant of the economy but the most important lever of power. Capture of the Bundesbank is thus, for them, the great prize in the European monetary war."

and gradually become a central bank more like that of Latin central banks. Actually, Southern Europe has control over the ECB. The council of the ECB is composed of the directors of the ECB and the presidents of the national central banks. All have the same vote. Germany and Northern, hard currency countries such as the Netherlands, Luxembourg and Belgium hold the minority of votes against countries like Italy, Portugal, Greece, Spain, and France, whose governments are less averse to deficits. These Latin countries had strong labor unions and high debts making them inherently prone to inflation.

The Euro was advantageous to Latin countries in that its inflation could be conducted without any direct evidence of an appreciating Deutschmark. Inflation would go on, but would be more hidden. When prices start to rise, it is relatively easy to blame it on certain industries. Politicians may, for instance, say that oil prices increase because of peak oil. But if oil prices go up and there is devaluation, it is more difficult for politicians to blame oil for the price increase. Devaluations coupled with higher inflation could easily lead to losses in elections. Devaluations against the Deutschmark disappeared with the introduction of the Euro.

Giscard d'Estaing, founder of a lobbying group for the Euro, stated in June 1992 that the ECB would finally put an end to the monetary supremacy of Germany.[2] What he meant was that the smoking gun that disciplined other countries would finally disappear. He added that the ECB should be used for macroeconomic growth policies; in other words, inflation. In a similar way, Jacques Attali, advisor to Mitterrand, acknowledged that the Maastricht Treaty was just a complicated contract whose purpose was to get rid of the Mark. This aim was also pursued by the Italians and others.[3]

PRESTIGE

With the ECB having been based on the model of the Bundesbank, high inflation countries inherited part of its prestige.

---

[2] Quoted in Baader, p. 207.

[3] Ibid., p. 208. See also Connolly, *The Rotten Heart of Europe*, p. 386.

The founding of the ECB was similar to an imaginary merger of the car makers Fiat and Daimler-Benz, where the Germans take over management and quality control. While the management majority is German, the Fiat's plants are still in Italy. The costs of undoing the merger, however, are immense. While it is certainly good for Fiat, it is not so good for Daimler-Benz itself.

The result of the introduction of the Euro was the expectation of a more stable currency for Southern European countries. Inflationary expectations fell in these countries. When inflation expectations are high, people reduce their cash holdings and start to buy as they think prices will be considerably higher in the future. When inflationary expectations fall, people increase their cash holdings marginally, leading to lower price inflation. This is one reason why rates of price inflation in the Southern countries went down even before the Euro was introduced. The expectation associated with the Euro reduced inflationary expectations, helping these countries to fulfil the Maastricht criterion of low inflation rates.

As in the case of a merger between Daimler and Fiat, for Germany, the Euro implied a watering down of the soundness of its currency. The fear for Germany was that the Euro would be less stable than the Deutschmark, spurring inflationary expectations. The German government was, in fact, using the Bundesbank's monetary prestige to the benefit of the inflationary member states and to the detriment of the general German population.

SOCIALIZED SEIGNORAGE

Some countries, especially France, made gains at the expense of the Germans due to a socialization of seignorage wealth.[4] Seignorage are the net profits resulting from the use of the printing press. When a central bank produces more base money,

---

[4] See Hans-Werner Sinn and Holger Feist, "Eurowinners and Eurolosers: The Distribution of Seignorage Wealth in the EU," *European Journal of Political Economy* 13 (1997): pp. 665–689. The socialization of seignorage income in the Eurosystem is laid down in Article 32 of the Protocol No. 18 on the Statute of the European System of Central Banks and of the European Central Banks of the Maastricht Treaty.

it buys assets, many of which yield income. For instance, a central bank may buy a government bond with newly produced money. The net interest income resulting from the assets is seignorage and transmitted at the end of the year to the government. As a result of the introduction of the Euro, seignorage was socialized in the EMU. Central banks had to send interest revenues to the ECB. The ECB would remit its own profits at the end of the year. One could imagine that this would be a zero sum game. But it is not. The ECB remits profits to national central banks based not on the assets held by individual central banks, but rather based on the capital that each central bank holds in the ECB. This capital, in turn, reflects population and GDP and not the national central banks' assets.

The Bundesbank, for instance, produced more base money in relation to its population and GDP than France, basically because the Deutschmark was an international reserve currency and was used in international transactions. The Bundesbank held more interest generating assets in relation to its population and GDP than France did. Consequently, the Bundesbank remitted relatively more interest revenues to the ECB than France, which were then redistributed to central banks based on population and GDP figures. While this scheme was disadvantageous for Germany, Austria, Spain and the Netherlands it was beneficial to France. Indeed, the Bundesbank profits remitted back to the German government fell after the introduction of the Euro. In the ten years before the single currency, the Bundesbank obtained €68.5 billion in profits. In the first ten years of the Euro the profit fell to €47.5 billion.

LOWER INTEREST RATES

The Euro lowered interest rates in the Southern countries, especially for government bonds. People and governments had to pay less interest on their debts. Investors bought the high yielding bonds of peripheral countries, which bid up their prices and brought down interest rates. This was a profitable deal because it could be expected that the bonds still denominated in Lira, Peseta, Escudo and Drachma would finally be paid back in Euros.

The lower interest rates allowed some countries to reduce their debt and fulfil the Maastricht criteria. Italy's rates, for instance, were reduced substantially, allowing the government to save on interest payments. In 1996, Italy paid around €110 billion in interest on its debts and in 1999, only around €79 billion.[5]

Southern interest rates were lowered for two main reasons. First, interest rates were reduced as inflationary expectations fell: the prestige of the Bundesbank partially transferred to the ECB led to lower interest payments. Second, the risk premium in rates was reduced. With the Euro, one currency was introduced as a step toward political integration in Europe. The Euro was installed supposedly for an indefinite period. The Eurozone's breakup was not provided for legally, and would be considered a huge political loss. The expectation was that stronger nations would bail out weaker nations if necessary.[6] With an implicit guarantee on their debts, many countries had to pay lower interest rates because the risk of default was reduced.

As Germany and other countries were implicitly guaranteeing for the debt of Mediterranean states, these states' lower interest rates were not in line with the real risk of default. The German government, in turn, had to pay higher interest rates on its debts than it would have paid otherwise; the danger of an additional burden was priced in. Markets normally punish budgetary indiscipline harshly, with higher interest rates and a depreciation of the currency. The European Monetary Union led to a delay of this punishment.

---

[5] Wilhelm Hankel, Wilhelm Nölling, Karl A. Schachtschneider and Joachim Starbatty, *Die Euro-Illusion. Warum Europa scheitern muß* (Hamburg: Rowohlt, 2001), p. 94.

[6] Theoretically, countries such as Greece could default without leaving the EMU. Yet, this would be considered a political catastrophe and would probably imply the end for any advancement toward a central European state.

As a consequence of the expected entry into the monetary union, interest rates converged to Germany's level, as can be seen in Graph 1. From 1995 on, it became more and more certain that Mediterranean countries (except Greece that participated in 2001) would participate in the monetary union in 1999.

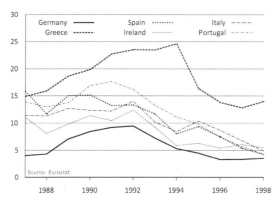

Graph 1: Three month monetary rates of interest in Germany, Greece, Spain, Ireland, Italy, and Portugal (1987–1998)

Rates fell even though real savings had not increased and because the inflation premium was reduced. The lower interest rates caused capital good prices to rise. As a consequence, a housing boom occurred in many Mediterranean countries. Credit was cheap and was used to buy and construct houses. This housing bubble was fed by expansionary monetary policy until 2008, when the global crisis lead to a crash in oversized housing markets.

MORE IMPORTS AND
A HIGHER LIVING STANDARD

High inflation states inherited a stronger currency from Germany and, consequently, could enjoy more imports and a higher standard of living. Even though Latin governments did not lower their expenditures significantly, the Euro remained relatively strong in international currency markets during the first years of its existence. The Euro was kept strong due to the prestige of the Bundesbank and the institutional setup of the

ECB, as well as due to strong German (and other Northern states) exports that increased the demand for Euros.

Germany has traditionally had current account surpluses, i.e., exports exceeding imports due to high efficiency and competitiveness. Germans saved and invested, improving productivity. At the same time, wage rates increased moderately. The resulting export surplus implied that Germans would travel to and invest in other countries. Germans acquired assets in foreign countries that could be sold in case of emergency. The result was an upwards pressure on the exchange rate.

Over the years, the Deutschmark tended to appreciate due to productivity increases in Germany. The Deutschmark became the symbol of the German economic miracle. The appreciation of the Deutschmark in foreign exchange markets made imports cheaper. Commodities and other inputs for the high quality German production process could be imported at lower prices. Also vacations and investments in foreign countries got cheaper. Living standards went up. This mechanism of increased productivity leading to more exports and tending toward an appreciation of the currency is still in place in the EMU.

But in the Southern EMU we have the opposite image. Production is less efficient there, relatively. Consumption rose in Southern Europe after the introduction of the Euro, and was spurred on by artificially lowered interest rates. Savings and investments have not increased as much as they have in Germany, and productivity increases have lagged behind. Moreover, new money has gone primarily to peripheral countries where it has pushed up wages. These wage increases have been higher than wage increases in Germany, leading to a loss in competitiveness, a surplus of imports over exports, and a tendency toward a depreciation of the currency. In addition, Southern governments were bribed by cash transfer payments in exchange for signing the Maastricht Treaty: "Jacques Delors, the Commission President, all but bribed the finance ministers if Greece, Spain, Portugal, and Ireland, promising large increases in EU structural funds in return for their signatures on the Treaty."[7] (Judt, *Postwar*, p. 715)

---

[7] See Judt, *Postwar*, p. 715. Conolly, *The Rotten Heart of Europe*, p. 198 writes:

As we can see in Graphs 2 and 3, competitiveness in Mediterranean countries and Ireland has decreased substantially since the introduction of the Euro. At the same time, competitiveness in Germany and even Austria has increased. Since the introduction of the Euro, Germany's competitiveness, as measured by the indicator based on unit labor costs provided by the ECB, increased 13.7 percent from the time of the Euro's introduction up until 2010. In the same period, Greece, Ireland, Spain, and Italy lost in competitiveness, 11.3, 9.1, 11.2, and 9.4 percent respectively.[8] According to the numbers provided by the ECB, Germany's competitive indicator of 88.8 in the first quarter of 2010 is substantially more competitive than Ireland with its 118.7, Greece with its 108.8, and Spain and Italy, with 111.6 each.

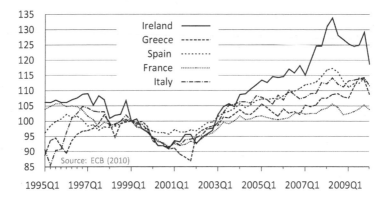

Graph 2: Competitiveness indicators based on unit labor costs, for Mediterranean countries and Ireland 1995–2010 (1999Q1=100)

"On 9 November 1991, the Irish, Spanish, Portuguese and Greek foreign ministers had left a meeting with Jacques Delors in which he had promised fabulous amounts (6 billion ECUs to Ireland) of other people's money if they pledged to support his federalist, corporatists ambitions in the final Maastricht negotiations."

[8] No data is provided for Portugal. It should be noted that we cannot take these data at face value as it may contain substantial errors. The data represent a very high level of aggregation. Nevertheless, the data may indicate tendencies.

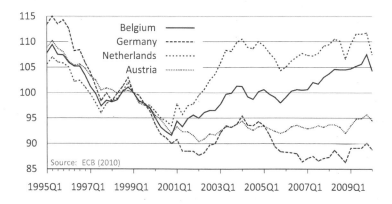

Graph 3: Competitiveness indicators based on unit labor costs, for Belgium, The Netherlands, Austria, and Germany 1995–2010 (1999Q1=100)

Before the introduction of the Euro, Latin countries with increasing wages, strong labor unions, and inflexible labor markets also lost competitiveness relative to Germany. Yet, before the single currency, inflations and devaluations regained competitiveness, lowering real wages. At the same time imports became more expensive.

When the Deutschmark was replaced by the Euro, Germany's export surplus was partially compensated for by import surpluses of Southern states. Trade surpluses and deficits of Eurozone states can be seen in Graph 4.

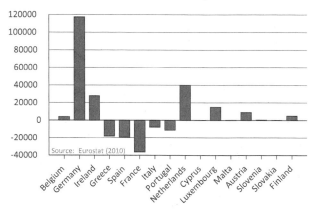

Graph 4: Balance of Trade 2009 (in million Euros)

In Graph 5 we see that Germany's trade surplus has increased in recent years due to the increase in competitiveness that comes along with an increased trade deficit of other countries. In fact, Germany's trade surplus more than compensates for the traditional trade deficits of Spain, Portugal, Italy, and Greece.

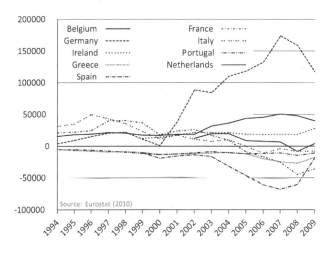

Graph 5: Balance of Trade 1994–2009 (in million Euros)

Long-lasting trade deficits drag negatively on the value of a currency. A trade deficit implies that there is a surplus in other parts of the balance of payments. There can be financial transfers toward the deficit country, or the country may increase its net position of foreign debts. Without sufficient financial transfers, a trade deficit implies that the public and private foreign debts of the country increase.

In this regard, it is not irrelevant if debts are held by a citizen or by a foreigner. Japanese government debts are held to a large extent by Japanese citizens and banks. Greek (or Spanish) government debts are largely held by foreign banks due to their trade deficits. Greeks did not save enough to buy their government debts, but preferred instead to import more goods and services than they exported. Foreign banks financed this consumption by buying Greek debts.

The Japanese government can force its banks to buy its government bonds or keep them from selling because they are within Japanese jurisdiction. The Greek government cannot force foreign banks to hold on to Greek government bonds. Neither can the Greek government force foreign banks to keep buying Greek debts in order to finance its deficit. If foreign banks stop buying or start selling Greek government bonds, the government may have to default. Trade deficits and resulting foreign debts make a currency vulnerable, while trade surpluses and net foreign positions make a currency stronger.

The development of the Euro pales when compared to what would have been the development of the Deutschmark alone. Imports and living standards in Germany did not increase as much as they would have with the Deutschmark. In fact, real retail sales in Germany lagged behind those in other industrial nations, as can be seen in Graph 6.

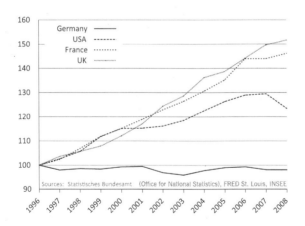

Graph 6: Retail sales in Germany, USA, France, and UK (1996=100)

But retail sales in Mediterranean countries increased and began to fall only with the economic crisis in 2008. From 2000 to 2007, retail sales in Spain increased more than twenty percent (Graph 7).

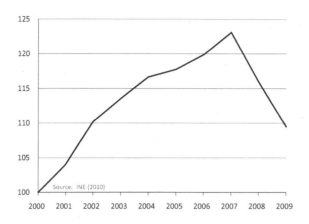

Graph 7: Retail sales in Spain (2000=100)

Imports remained cheaper for Southern Europe than they probably would have without the monetary union. Even though inflationary countries lost competitiveness relative to Germany, imports did not increase in price as much as they would have had these countries relied on their own currencies. The result of combining this with artificially low interest rates was the credit-financed consumption boom, especially in the Southern states.

AN EXCUSE FOR BUDGET CUTS

Southern European politicians used the Maastricht Treaty as an excuse (before a socialist constituency) for deregulation and taking budgetary saving measures necessary to prevent bankruptcy. In order to fulfil the convergence criteria, Southern countries had to reduce their deficits, cut government spending, and sell public companies. For many countries, in fact, the Euro was the only prospect for delaying sovereign default or hyper-inflation. Public debts pressed European welfare states severely before the introduction of the Euro. In 1991 Belgium, Ireland and Italy had debts of 132%, 113%, and 103% of the GDP.[9] Even

---

[9] Baader, *Die Euro-Katastrophe,* p. 204. Without the implicit German guarantee the debt situation of Belgium would have been unsustainable. See Connolly, *The Rotten Heart of Europe,* p. 344.

the Netherlands had a debt of 83% of the GDP, with Greece not far behind. In the end, the issue of a single currency was about power and money and not about high-minded European thinking.

GAINS THROUGH
MONETARY REDISTRIBUTION

When the Euro was introduced, it did not take long for imbalances to develop and accumulate. The current account deficit in Southern states increased in a consumption boom and the German export industry flourished. An appreciation of the Deutschmark would have caused problems for German exporters and reduced the current account surplus of Germany. With the Euro, this was no longer possible.

New Euros flew from the credit induced boom in Southern countries into Germany and pushed up prices there. Redistributions occurred as the ECB continued to finance and accommodate consumption spending in these countries. New money would enter the Southern countries and buy German products.

In Graph 8, we can see the growth of M3 (excluding circulating currency) in Spain, Italy, Greece, Portugal, and Germany. We see that the money supply indeed grew much faster in the Mediterranean countries. Spain and Greece, especially, had faster growth rates than Germany did (thick line) during the boom years of the early 2000s until 2008. For instance, when Germany's monetary aggregate was falling in 2002, Spain and Italy had double digit increases. In 2004, Germany's growth of money aggregates was hovering at two percent. Monetary growth was at least double in the Mediterranean countries at the same time. When Spain's housing boom got out of control in 2007, M3 grew to twenty percent while Germany's aggregate grew between five and eight percent.

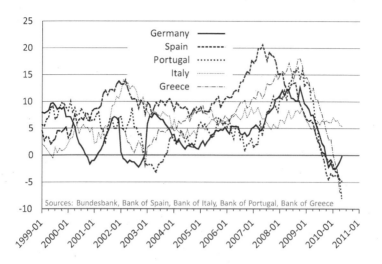

Graph 8: Increase in M3 in percent (without currency in circulation) in Spain, Germany, Italy, Greece, and Portugal (1999–2010)

The redistribution through different rates in money production brought on a culture of decadence. This development resembled the "curse of gold" that Spain experienced after the discovery of the New World, when new money, i.e., gold, would flow in to the country. Spain would then import goods and services (mostly military) from the rest of Europe. As a consequence, European exporters would experience profits and Spanish industry would become ever more inefficient.

The same has happened in the Eurozone. Money was injected at a faster rate in Southern states. After constructing houses, money spread to the rest of the Eurozone as Spain imported goods from Germany and other Northern countries. The Mediterranean current account deficit increased.

If the monetary injection had been a one time event only, the situation would have soon stabilized. Prices would have increased in Germany relative to the Southern countries as Euros bought German goods. Lower prices and wages in the Southern countries would have made these countries more efficient and reduced the current account deficit.

But this readjustment was not allowed to happen. New money continued to flow more quickly into Mediterranean states where it was passed on to Southern consumers and governments, keeping prices from falling (prices that were relatively higher than those in Germany). The flow of goods from Germany to the Southern countries continued. The current account deficit was maintained and Southern countries stayed relatively unproductive while becoming accustomed to a level of consumption that would not have been possible without the money creation in their favor. Southern inflation was exported to Germany while monetary stability was imported. Southern prices did not rise as much as they would have without the imports from Germany. German prices increased more than they would have without the exports to Southern Europe.

In a form of monetary imperialism, banks and governments in Southern countries produced money that Germans had to accept.[10] Take an example: the Greek central bank prints money to finance the salary of a Greek politician. The Greek politician buys a Mercedes. (The politician may buy a tank. With a population of eleven million, Greece is the largest importer of conventional weapons in Europe. Military spending in Greece captures the highest percentage of the GDP of all countries in the EU.)

In a gold standard, gold would leave Greece and flow to Germany in exchange for imported goods. In fluctuating fiat paper currencies, a politician would have to exchange his newly printed Drachma into Deutschmark; the Deutschmark would rise in value and the next vacation of the German automobile worker in Greece would be less expensive. In the case of the Euro, paper money flows into Germany where it is accepted as legal tender and bids up prices.

---

[10] On monetary nationalism see Hans-Hermann Hoppe, "Banking, Nation States, and International Politics: A Sociological Reconstruction of the Present Economic Order," *Review of Austrian Economics* 4 (1, 1990): pp. 55–87.

CHAPTER FIVE

Why Germany Gave Up
the Deutschmark

If the Euro means so many disadvantages for Germany, how is it possible that Germany agreed to its introduction? The fact is, the majority of the population wanted to keep the Deutschmark (some polls say up to seventy percent of Germans wanted to keep the Deutschmark). Why did politicians not listen to majority opinion?

The most feasible explanation is that the German government sacrificed the Deutschmark in order to make way for reunification in 1990. When the Wall came down, unification negotiations began. The negotiators included the two Germanys and the winning allies of World War II: the UK, the US, France, and the Soviet Union.

Germany was still subject to domination. No peace treaty was signed with Germany after World War II. The Potsdam Agreement of August, 1945, stipulated that a peace treaty would be signed once an adequate government was established. But such a treaty was never signed. Germany did not enjoy full sovereignty because allies had special control rights until the commencement of the Two Plus Four Agreement in 1991.[1]

---

[1] The UN Charter still contains enemy state clauses. The clauses allow the allies to impose measures against states such as Germany or Japan without authorization of the Security Council. "[T]he allies reserved certain powers of interventions and even the right to resume direct rule if they judged it necessary." (Judt, *Postwar*, p. 147).

In 1990, the Soviet Union still had troops stationed in Eastern Germany, while the United States, France, and Great Britain commanded troops in the Western part. All four of the occupying forces were atomic powers and vastly superior to Germany militarily. Without the authorization of these four powers, a unification of Germany would not have been possible. The French and British governments in particular feared the power of a unified Germany, which could easily demand its natural place in the power structure of Europe: it is the most populated nation, the strongest economically, and it is located in the strategic heart of Europe.[2]

To curb this power, the Two Plus Four Agreement, or Treaty on the Final Settlement With Respect to Germany, specified that the German government had to give up all claims on the territories taken from it after World War II. Moreover, Germany had to pay twenty-one billion Deutschmarks to the Soviet Union for pulling its troops out of the Eastern part.[3] The German government had to reduce the size of its military and renew its renunciation of the possession or control over nuclear, biological, and chemical weapons.

Much more feared than the German army—made up primarily of infantry destined to slow down a Soviet attack on NATO—was the Bundesbank. The Bundesbank repeatedly forced other nations to curtail their printing presses or to realign their foreign exchange rates. It seems possible, if not plausible, that Germany had to give up the Deutschmark and monetary sovereignty in exchange for unification.[4] Former German

---

[2] As Margaret Thatcher states on Mitterrand and herself: "[W]e both had the will to check the German juggernaut." Quoted in Judt, *Postwar*, p. 639.

[3] Fritjof Meyer, "Ein Marshall auf einem Sessel," *Der Spiegel* 40 (1999): p. 99, http://www.spiegel.de. Germany paid sixty-three billion Deutschmarks to the Soviet Union from 1989 to 1991 (in total) in order to receive favorable treatment. Similarly Tony Judt, *Postwar*, p. 642, calculates that the German government transferred $71 billion to the Soviet Union from 1990 to 1994. Additional $36 billion of "tributes" flew to other former Communist governments of Eastern Europe.

[4] See Kerstin Löffler, "Paris und London öffnen ihre Archive," Ntv.de (November 6, 2010), http://n-tv.de. See also Wilhelm Nölling quoted in Hannich, *Die kommende Euro-Katastrophe*, p. 21: "As far as we know, these countries demanded in exchange for the agreement to reunification . . . that they could

President, Richard von Weizsäcker, claimed that the Euro would be "nothing else than the price of the reunification."[5] Former foreign secretary Hans-Dietrich Genscher stated upon the introduction of the Euro that the events constituted the payment of promises made by him during the process of German unification.[6] Similarly, German politician Norbert Blüm stated that Germany had to make sacrifices, namely the Deutschmark, for the newly shaped Europe.[7] Horst Teltschik,[8] chief foreign policy adviser of Chancellor Helmut Kohl, quoted himself, telling a French journalist (three weeks after the Berlin Wall came down in 1989) that "the German Federal Government was now in a position that it had to accept practically any French initiative for Europe."[9]

Kohl regarded the Euro as a question of war and peace. After reunification, Kohl wanted to construct a politically unified Europe around France and Germany. Kohl wanted to gain his place in the history books as a builder of German reunification and a political union in Europe.[10] In order to succeed, he needed the collaboration of the French President, Mitterrand.

---

not prevent, that Germany would be captivated and to do this there is nothing better in addition to NATO and European integration than to unify also the currency." In a speech in August 2010 historian Heinrich August Winkler, professor emeritus at Humboldt University Berlin, argued that Mitterrand feared that the European Community would turn into a Deutschmark zone implying German hegemony on the continent. The Euro was the price for the reunification. See Henkel, *Rettet unser Geld!*, pp. 56–58. Access to secret protocols has recently validated the thesis that Mitterrand demanded the single currency for his agreement to unification. See Mik, "Mitterrand forderte Euro als Gegenleistung für die Einheit, Spiegel online (2010), http://www.spiegel.de.

[5] In Die Woche, September 19, 1997 quoted in "Die Risiken des Euro sind unübersehbar (1)," in *Das Weisse Pferd – Urchristliche Zeitung für Gesellschaft, Religion, Politik und Wirtschaft* (August, 1998), http://www.das-weisse-pferd.com.

[6] See Henkel, *Rettet unser Geld!*, p. 59.

[7] See Hannich, *Die kommende Euro-Katastrophe.*

[8] Horst Teltschik, *329 Tage: Innenansichten der Einigung* (Berlin: Siedler, 1991), p. 61,

[9] Vaubel, "The Euro and the German Veto," p. 83.

[10] Kohl was considered a candidate for the Nobel Peace Prize several times, most recently in 2010.

Former translator for Mitterrand, Brigitte Sauzay, writes in her memoirs that Mitterrand would only agree to the German reunification "if the German chancellor sacrificed the Mark for the Euro."[11] Jacques Attali, adviser to Mitterrand, made similar remarks in a TV interview in 1998:

> It is thanks to French reticence with regard to an un-conditional reunification [of Germany] that we have the common currency . . . . The common currency would not have been created without the reticence of François Mitterrand regarding German unification.

Another confirmation of these events is provided by Hubert Védrine, also a long time adviser to Mitterrand, and later his minister for foreign affairs:

---

[11] Spiegel-Special Nr. 2/1998 quoted in *Das Weisse Pferd*, "Die Risiken des Euro." For the view that the French government agreed to reunification in ex-change for an agreement of the German one on the introduction of a single currency see also Ginsberg, *Demystifying the European Union*, p. 249. Similarly, Jonas Ljundberg, "Introduction," in *The Price of the Euro*, ed. Jonas Ljundberg (New York: Palgrave MacMillan, 2004), p. 10, states: "By relinquishing *Bundesbank* hegemony among the central banks Kohl could secure the compliance of Mitterrand for the German reunification." In the same line, James Foreman-Peck, "The UK and the Euro: Politics versus Economics in a Long-Run Per-spective," in *The Price of the Euro*, ed. Jonas Ljundberg (New York: Palgrave MacMillan, 2004), p. 102, states: "Monetary union was chosen instead as part of a Franco-German deal over German reunification. The Deutschmark was traded in for a unified state. This large, united Germany needed to be accep-table to France, and monetary union was the price charged by the French government." He adds (Foreman-Peck, p. 114): " . . . the Euro was agreed to allow more French control of European monetary policy than under the *Bundesbank* in return for French acceptance of German reunification." Larsson ("National Policy in Disguise," p. 163) states: "The EMU became an oppor-tunity for the French to get a share of the German economic power. For the German Federal Chancellor Kohl, the EMU was an instrument to make the other EC member states accept the German reunion and consequently a larger and stronger Germany in the heart of Europe." Judt (*Postwar*, p. 640) states: "The Germans could have their unity, but at a price . . . Kohl must commit himself to pursuing the European project under a Franco-German condomi-nium [Bonn paying and Paris making the policies], and Germany was to be bound into a 'ever-closer' union – whose terms, notably a common European currency, would be enshrined in a new treaty."

The President knew to grasp the opportunity, at the end of 1989, to obtain a commitment from [German Chancellor Helmut] Kohl. [. . .] Six months later, it would have been too late: no French President would have still been in a position to obtain from a German Chancellor the commitment to introduce the common currency.[12]

François Mitterrand and Margaret Thatcher were horrified by the idea of a unified, "strong" Germany. Germany had to lose its keenest weapon. Neighbors were worried about a renewed German aggression. The monetary union was the solution to this threat, as Mitterrand said to Thatcher after the German unification: "Without a common currency we are all—you and we—under German rule. When they raise their interest rates, we have to follow and you do the same, even though you do not participate in our currency system. We can only join in if there is a European Central Bank where we decide together."[13]

THE ROLE OF THE FRENCH GOVERNMENT

France was militarily and politically the most powerful nation on the European continent west of the Iron Curtain after World War II. France's leaders used this leverage to gain influence over European institutions and reduce the political influence of its eternal rival Germany. Indeed, France is overrepresented in the EU in term of the size of its population and GDP in relation to Germany.[14] The French government had always wanted to get rid of the influence of the Bundesbank.[15] A single

---

[12] Both quotations are taken from Vaubel, "The Euro and the German Veto," pp. 82–83.

[13] Translated from quote in Hannich, *Die kommende Euro-Katastrophe*, p. 22. As Connolly, *The Rotten Heart of Europe*, p. 142 writes: "Leading French Socialists . . . had all implied that only the Maastricht Treaty could hold the 'old demons' of the German character in check."

[14] See Larsson, "National Policy in Disguise." Germany is underrepresented not only in relation to France. In the Council Germany has twenty-nine votes, the same as United Kingdom, France, and Italy that all are substantially smaller in population and GDP. Spain and Poland, with about half of the population of Germany, each have twenty-seven votes.

[15] Bernard Connolly, The *Rotten Heart of Europe*, p. 100 writes: "In French eyes,

currency was seen as an opportunity to reinforce its position and steer Europe toward an empire led by the French ruling class. France's own central bank was under the direct control of the government until 1993 and was used as an instrument to pay for government expenditures. The Bundesbank was a hindrance to these endeavors. The Bank of France wanted to spur growth via credit expansion. But because the more independent Bundesbank did not inflate to the same extent, France had to devaluate several times.

The Bundesbank put a break on French inflation. The Deutschmark was, in a sense, the new standard in the wake of gold. Its power came from its less inflationary stand when compared to most other European central banks. It came from its independence and resistance to calls for inflation by the German government. When the Bundesbank raised interest rates, the Bank of France had to follow suit if it did not want the Franc to depreciate and to have to realign.

From the French point of view, however, German policies were not sufficiently inflationary; French politicians opposed the lead of the Bundesbank. Though militarily weak and a loser of World War II, Germany was able to dictate interest rates and indirectly restrict French government spending: an éclat.[16] Mitterrand remarked to his Council of Ministers in 1988: "Germany is a big nation that lacks some characteristics of sovereignty and enjoys a reduced diplomatic status. Germany compensates for its weakness through economic strength. The Deutschmark is in a way its atomic force."[17]

---

the point of EMU, in monetary terms at least, was to get French hands on the Bundesbank."

[16] As Connolly (*The Rotten Heart of Europe*, p. 30) wrote commenting on developments of 1983: "French wage and budget policy had already ended up being set by Germany . . . The humiliation for the French Socialist government was near total, a sort of monetary 1940." Trichet experienced another humiliation later. (Ibid, p. 311.)

[17] Quoted in Hannich, *Die kommende Euro-Katastrophe*, p. 22, and Marsh, *Der Euro*, p. 175. Also Mitterrand's predecessor, Valéry Giscard d'Estaing, feared a German hegemony. See Marsh, *Der Euro*, p. 99. See also Feldstein, "The Political Economy of the European Political and Monetary Union," p. 28, who states that France used the EMU to bolster its influence vis-à-vis Germany.

Moreover, the French government held that a central bank should support its government in its actions. In the case of high unemployment, for example, the central bank should cut interest rates irrespective of inflationary pressure. In a common central bank that included the Mediterranean countries, Germany would be in the minority and French politicians could determine its course. Malta has the same vote in the ECB as Germany does, for instance, even though Germany has a GDP 500 times that of Malta. A common currency with a common central bank was a long term political aim of the French government for which it was willing to sacrifice short term ends.[18]

Mitterrand, France's president from 1981 to 1995, had hated Germany in his youth and despised capitalism.[19] The French patriot was a staunch defender of the socialist vision of Europe and geared his policies toward defending France against the economic superiority of its Eastern neighbor. Germany's superiority was based on its currency. Mitterrand's intention was to use Germany's monetary power for the interest of the French government.[20] The French government could give the Germans security guarantees in exchange for participation in Germany's monetary power. When speaking of French short range atomic bombs that could only explode in Germany at the end of the 1980s, Mitterrand's foreign adviser Jacques Attali, to the surprise of the German negotiators, alluded to a German

---

[18] Connolly, *The Rotten Heart of Europe*, p. 146, argues that Southern central bankers and politicians agreed to restrictive monetary policies in order to attain the long term end of the single currency and to be able to outvote Bundesbankers: "Their [Southern elites] greatest desire might be to find themselves in a position where they could overrule Schlesinger [former President of the Bundesbank], or rather his successors, but they would only ever get there if, in the meantime, the central bankers' club did not break ranks."

[19] See Marsh, *Der Euro*, pp. 47–50. He explicitly stated that he wanted a clean break with capitalism. (Connolly, *The Rotten Heart of Europe*, p. 24.)

[20] See Marsh, *Der Euro*, p. 57. In a similar language Jacques Delors was indignant over the Bundesbank when it did not reduce interest rates in 1993 to support the franc: "Why have they declared war on us?" (Quoted in Connolly, *The Rotten Heart of Europe*, p. 321.)

atomic bomb: the Deutschmark.[21] The French government tried to use its military strength to gain monetary concessions.[22]

With the unification of Germany, the opponents of the Deutschmark could pressure the German government to give it up. First Mitterrand wanted to block German unification altogether: "I don't have to do anything to stop it; the Soviets will do it for me. They will never allow this greater Germany just opposite them."[23] When the Soviet Union did not stop it, Mitterrand seized the opportunity and saw in Kohl an ally of the Euro.[24] He feared that once Kohl resigned, the German government could threaten the peace in Europe once again. Both politicians regarded a common currency as the means to restoring European political equilibrium after reunification. European politicians in general thought that a monetary union would control the rising power of a unified Germany. Giscard d'Estaing claimed that a failure of the monetary union would lead to a German hegemony in Europe.[25]

---

[21] Hannich, *Die kommende Euro-Katastrophe,* p. 22. Marsh, *Der Euro,* pp. 172–174

[22] Similar implicit threats occurred in 1992 in a crisis of the French franc. On this occasion, Trichet called the Franco-German reconciliation into question in order to get support from Germany. When asked why the minimum reserve requirements German banks had to hold with the Bundesbank could not be increased to restrict inflationary pressures, a Bundesbanker answered: "Because if we did that the sky would be dark with the squadrons of Mirages coming across the Rhine to bomb us" (Quoted in Connolly, *The Rotten Heart of Europe,* p. 180.)

[23] Quoted in Judt, *Postwar,* p. 637.

[24] Bandulet, *Die letzten Jahre des Euro,* p. 48. Most probably, Mitterrand was only bluffing. He was not in a position to prevent the reunification even if Kohl would not have sacrificed the Mark. Neither the United States nor the Soviet Union pressured the German government to sign the Maastricht Treaty as a condition for reunification.

[25] See Marsh, *Der Euro,* p. 263. The Italian Prime Minister Andreotti warned of a new Pan-Germanism. Netherlands' Prime Minister Lubbers was against the reunification as was Thatcher, who took two maps of Germany out of her bag at a summit in Strasbourg. One map was Germany before, the other after World War II. She stated that Germany would take back all of its lost territories plus Czechoslovakia. See Marsh, *Der Euro,* p. 203. On the French preoccupation with German hegemony in Europe see also Connolly, *The Rotten Heart of Europe,* p. 88 or p. 384.

Tensions intensified when Kohl did not acknowledge the borders of the unified Germany and Poland, which had gained substantial territory from Germany after World War II. Mitterrand demanded a common currency, fearing that the world would otherwise return to its state of 1913.[26] In response to this massive threat and the looming isolation between an alliance of France, Great Britain and the Soviet Union, Kohl agreed to set a date for a conference on a common currency in the second half of 1990. He even stated that the single currency would be a matter of war and peace. Kohl's agreeing to a plan toward the introduction of a common currency at last placated France's fear of a unified Germany.

ADVANTAGES FOR
THE GERMAN RULING CLASS

The sacrifice of the Deutschmark was quite to the liking of the German ruling class. As Hans-Hermann Hoppe has pointed out, there is a ruling class in our societies that uses the state as a device for the exploitation of the rest of the population.[27] The state is the monopolist of coercion and the ultimate decision maker in all conflicts in a given territory. It has the power to tax and make all manner of interventions.

The ruling class is exploitive, parasitic, unproductive, and has a strong class consciousness. It needs an ideology to justify its actions and prevent rebellion of the exploited class. The exploited class represents the majority, produces wealth, is indoctrinated into obedience to the ruling class, and has no special class consciousness.

Every state has its own ruling class and connected interest groups. Consequently, the ruling class in Germany and the ruling class in France may have more in common than the German ruling class and the exploited class in Germany. In fact, the German ruling and exploited classes have opposite interests. But there are many areas in which the French and German

---

[26] See Marsh, *Der Euro*, p. 202.

[27] See Hans-Hermann Hoppe, "Marxist and Austrian Class Analysis," *Journal of Libertarian Studies* 9 (2, 1990): pp. 79–93.

ruling classes are not competitors and actually may benefit from working together. Both ruling classes want power: they want to expand their power vis-à-vis their citizens. They want an ideology to prevail that favors the state and an increase in the state's power.

Given the above considerations, it is easy to understand why the German ruling class, i.e., politicians, banks, and connected industries, especially exporters, favored the introduction of the Euro. There were many ways it could benefit from a single currency.

1. The ruling class most likely did not regret getting rid of the very conservative Bundesbank. The Bundesbank had acted several times against the interests and pleas of politicians. It raised interest rates before elections in 1969, for instance, increasing its reputation as an anti-inflation central bank worldwide. In addition, the Bundesbank did not want to follow the inflation rates of the US and stopped interventions in favor of the dollar in March of 1973. This led to the final collapse of the Bretton Woods System and fluctuating exchange rates. It also resisted the establishment of an obligation to intervene in the EMS. Bundesbankers repeatedly resisted demands made by German and foreign politicians for a reduction of interest rates. Some Bundesbankers were also sceptical about the introduction of the Euro as an instrument toward economic integration. Leading German politicians often had the burden of dealing with the discontent of their neighbors due to the uncompromising monetary stance of the Bundesbank.[28]

The Euro allowed German politicians to rid themselves of stubborn Bundesbankers, promising the end of the bank's "tyranny." More inflation would mean more power for the ruling class. German politicians would be

---

[28] See Vaubel, "A Critical Analysis of EMU and of Sweden Joining It." See also extensively Connolly, *The Rotten Heart of Europe,* for instance p. 205. The German government repeatedly tried to influence the Bundesbank out of political reasons.

able to hide behind the ECB and flee the responsibility of high debts and expenditures.

The Euro was a step toward the establishment of a world currency. With all currency competition eliminated, politicians would have unlimited power.[29] Moreover, international monetary cooperation is easier to achieve between the Fed and the ECB than it would be between the Fed and several European central banks.

2. Certain German interest groups stood to make gains for themselves, namely, an "advancement" of European integration including the harmonization of labor, environmental and technological standards.[30] Indeed, the introduction of the Euro saved the European project of a centralization of state power.

The harmonization of labor standards benefited German unionized workers. High labor standards in Germany were possible due to the high productivity of German workers. Workers in other countries such as Portugal or Greece had less capital with which to work, making them less productive. In order to compete with the German worker, the Portuguese needed lower labor standards, which reduced the cost of their labor. The lowering of labor standards—widely feared as "a race to the bottom"—threatened the high labor standards of German workers. Unionized German workers complying with high labor standards did not want to compete with Portuguese workers for whom compliance was not required. The competitive advantage gained by the harmonization of standards would give German unions leeway to extend their power and privileges.

The harmonization of environmental standards also benefited German companies because they were already the

---

[29] For the U.S. interests pushing for a world central bank see Murray Rothbard, *Wall Street, Banks, and American Foreign Policy* (Auburn, Ala.: Ludwig von Mises Institute, 1995).

[30] Guido Hülsmann, "Political Unification: A Generalized Progression Theorem," *Journal of Libertarian Studies* 13 (1, 1997): pp. 81–96.

most efficient environmentally. Competing companies from other countries with lower standards had to adopt these more costly standards. Moreover, Green interests were satisfied by the imposition of German environmental standards on the rest of the European Union. German companies were leading in environmental and other technologies and profiting from this regulation. Imposing German technological standards in the EU gave German exporters a competitive advantage.

3. German exporters benefited from an inflationary Euro in a dual way. Other Eurozone countries could no longer devalue their currency to gain competitiveness. In fact, currency crises and sudden devaluations had endangered German exporters. A currency crisis also put the common market in jeopardy. With a single currency, devaluation would no longer be possible. Italian Prime Minister Romani Prodi employed this argument to convince German politicians to allow a debt-ridden Italy to join the monetary union: support our membership and we'll buy your exports.[31]

In addition, budget and trade deficits of Southern countries made the Euro consistently weaker than the Deutschmark would have been. Higher German exports were compensated for by trade deficits of uncompetitive member states. As a consequence, German exporters had an advantage over countries outside the Eurozone. Increases in productivity would not translate into appreciations of the currency, at least not when compared to the Deutschmark.

4. The German political class wanted to avoid political and financial collapse.[32]

Many countries in Europe were on the verge of bankruptcy in the 1990s. As the ruling class did not want to lose power, it was willing to give up some control of the printing press

---

[31] See James Neuger, "Euro Breakup Talk Increases as Germany Loses Proxy," *Bloomberg* (May 14, 2010), http://www.bloomberg.com.

[32] See Hülsmann, "Political Unification," for the political centralization theorem.

in exchange for survival. Countries with less debt such as Germany would guarantee the confidence of creditors, so that the overall level of European debt could be maintained or even expanded. This certainly explains the interest of highly indebted countries at the verge of bankruptcy in European integration.

The ruling class can extend its power by increasing taxes, using inflation, or through higher debts. But taxes are unpopular. Inflation also becomes disruptive when at some point citizens flee into real values and the monetary system is in danger of collapse. Debts are an alternative to financing higher spending and power and they are not as unpopular as taxes. In fact, there may be a "government bonds illusion." Citizens may well feel richer if government expenditures are financed through bonds instead of through taxes. Nevertheless, they have to be financed at some point via inflation or taxes, lest creditors close the overly indebted government's money stream.

But why would Germany take on the role of guarantor?

Introducing the Euro and implicitly guaranteeing for the debts of the other nations came along with direct and indirect transfers of the Eurosystem.[33] Bankruptcy of the

---

[33] Daniel K. Tarullo, "International Response to European Debt Problems," Testimony Before the Subcommittee on International Monetary Policy and Trade and Subcommittee on Domestic Monetary Policy and Technology, Committee on Financial Services, U.S. House of Representatives, Washington, D.C. (May 20, 2010), http://www.federalreserve.gov. As Daniel Tarullo, member of the board of the Federal Reserve, stated: "For years many market participants had assumed that an implicit guarantee protected the debt of euro-area members." For similar perception of the implicit bailout guarantee see John Browne, "Euro Fiasco Threatens the World," *Triblive* (July 18, 2010), http://www. pittsburghlive.com, and Robert Samuelson, "Greece and the Welfare State in Ruins," *Real Clear Politics* (February 22, 2010), http://www.realclearpolitics. com. This perception started to change when the debts of governments in the periphery of the EMU started to soar during the crisis. German politicians signaled problems with a bailout. At this point the yield of Greek bonds rose relative to the yield of German ones, reflecting the true risk of default.

European states, which would have had adverse effects on the German ruling class, could be averted, at least for some time. A collapse of one or several countries would lead to recession. Due to the international division of labor in Europe, a recession would hit big exporters and established companies even in Germany. Tax revenues would fall and the support of the population would be reduced.

Moreover, the default of a country would probably affect negatively the domestic banking system and have a domino effect on banks all over Europe, including Germany. The connectivity of the international financial system might lead to the collapse of German banks, close allies of the German ruling class, and strong supporters of a single currency. A bankruptcy in form of hyperinflation would equally negatively affect international trade and the financial system. Sovereign bankruptcies could take governments down with them.

In sum, the introduction of the Euro was not about a European ideal of liberty and peace. On the contrary, the Euro was not necessary for liberty and peace. In fact, the Euro produced conflict. Its introduction was all about power and money. The Euro brought the most important economic power tool, the monetary unit, under the control of technocrats.

CHAPTER SIX

The Money Monopoly of the ECB

Let us for a moment ponder the sheer power the ECB exerts on the life of the people in the European Monetary Union (EMU). It is a power that no institution would amass in a free society. Even though the immense concentration of power of Soviet times is of the past, the ECB still exerts total control over the monetary sphere; it has the power to create money and to thereby help mould the fate of society.

Imagine you had the power the ECB has. You would be the only person producing money; let us say you could just print it with your PC; or more simply, you could access your bank account online and add any sum to it you want. Everybody would have to accept the money you produce. You would have a power comparable to that of Tolkien's ring. Would you use this power? The temptation is almost irresistible. You might actually try to use it to do good. But the result of this setup would be a permanent flow of goods and services to you, your family, and friends, in exchange for the newly produced money. This would lead to a tendency for prices to increase. If you wanted to buy a BMW, you would produce new money. Then you would have to overbid the person that would have bought it had you not produced additional money. Prices are bid up. Now you get the BMW and this other person does not. The dealer may now use the additional money and buy a coat for his wife, bidding up prices of coats. The coat producer's income is higher and he starts spending. Gradually, the new money extends through the economy, increasing prices and changing the stream of goods and services toward the first receivers of the new money.

While the use of the power of the printing press is virtually irresistible, you have to be careful not to overdo it—for several reasons.

People might start to resist the scheme and try to destroy your power. When they see that you just have to print money and you get richer and they get poorer, they may revolt. Before it gets to this point you may want to restrict your money production. But there are other means of diluting this source of unrest and resistance. You could develop a strategy that conceals the money creation and creates diversions. You may transfer the new funds through several steps in an intricate system whose mechanisms are hard to grasp. (We will see shortly how the ECB does it.) You may also try to convince people that the scheme is actually good for them. You may claim that what you are doing will stabilize the price level, or that you are altruistically trying to spur employment. (These are, by the way, the official ends of the ECB.)

People may actually start to like you and claim that without you, the financial system would collapse. Concentrate in your argumentation on an important consequence of your money creation instead of the money creation itself: say that you control interest rates for the best of society. In other words, focus on the effect of your policies (changes in interest rates, for example) and not on what you are doing to manipulate interest rates (producing money). Claim that you are lowering interest rates to make more investments and employment possible. Use metaphors: your money production is the lubricating oil necessary for the smooth functioning of the economy. Develop theories supporting your scheme. Hire economists to support you and develop the corresponding monetary theories, even though their extravagance (flights, cars, and parties) cost you a few (new) bucks (or Euros).[1] One of things you may argue is that what you are doing is necessary to prevent the disster of falling prices. Another is that the banking system needs new money and would otherwise collapse—with apocalyptic consequences. You have achieved your end when victims and losers of the scheme actually start to think that you are doing them some good by producing money.

Now you must be careful not to disturb the economy too much by your money production. You do not want too much chaos. You will still want to be able to buy a BMW and enjoy some technological progress. If people stop saving and investing due to inflation, car production will not continue. If uncertainty increases too much, you will have to forgo many advantages. If the newly produced money causes too many disturbances and distortions in the form of business cycles, productivity will be hampered, and this might not be in your best interest. Surely, you want neither hyperinflation nor a collapse of the monetary system. No one would want your newly printed money anymore. Your power would be gone.

As mentioned before, it is also in your interest to cover your tracks. This can be done by erecting a complicated financial system that is hard to understand. You may give privileges to some in exchange for their eternal friendship and help. The privilege consists in letting them participate in your monopoly; giving them some sort of franchise in auxiliary money production. These individuals, we may call them fractional reserve bankers, cannot print money themselves, but if they hold money reserves with you, they will be allowed to produce money substitutes—demand deposits, for example—on top of these reserves. Let us look at a simple example to show how the franchise system works. Let us assume you (the central

---

[1] The Fed is quite good at it. As Lawrence White shows, in 2002 some seventy-four percent of all academic writings on monetary theory were published in Fed-published journals or co-authored by Fed staff economists. (Lawrence White, "The Federal Reserve System's Influence on Research in Monetary Economics," Econ Journal Watch 2 (2005): pp. 325–354.)

bank) print €100.000 to buy a BMW. After your purchase, the car dealer deposits the money in bank A. The balance sheet of bank A reads as follows.

Debit		Credit	
Cash	€100.000	Deposit from BMW dealer	€100.000

The bank holds one hundred percent reserves of the deposit from the BMW dealer who deposited the money with intent of having full availability of the money. According to general legal principles, it is then the obligation of the bank to hold the money in safekeeping, making it at any time available. The money supply in our example is now the cash created by the central bank to which the dealer holds the deposit, a monetary substitute: €100.000. Imagine that we now give our friend, bank A, the privilege of holding only ten percent reserves instead of safekeeping the money. This implies that the bank can buy assets (loans or houses, etc.) and pay with newly created deposits. In other words, the bank can make loans to a person and put new money in the bank account of this person.

Debit		Credit	
Cash	€100.000	Deposit from BMW dealer	€100.000
Loan to person U	€90.000	Deposit of person U	€90.000

The bank has created €90.000 out of thin air and put it into the bank account of U. When U now uses the money completely, for instance, purchasing a good from person V, the cash reserves of bank A fall to €10.000. The deposit of U disappears. Bank maintains a reserve ratio of 10 percent.

The balance sheet of bank A remains:

Debit		Credit	
Cash	€10.000	Deposit from BMW dealer	€100.000
Loan to person U	€90.000		

Let us now imagine that person V is client of bank B and deposits the €90.000 in this bank. Now, bank B can expand credits. Holding a reserve ratio of 10 percent, bank B may grant a loan of €81.000 to person W.

Debit		Credit	
Cash	€90.000	Deposit from V	€90.000
Loan to person W	€81.000	Deposit of person W	€81.000

Now, W can use his loan, get the money from his bank account and transfer it to person X for purchasing a good or service. After this operation, the balance sheet of bank B is as follows:

Debit		Credit	
Cash	€9.000	Deposit from person V	€90.000
Loan to person W	€81.000		

X is client of bank C and puts his money (€81.000) into it. Bank C has now received new cash reserves and can create new money and grant a loan to person Y. Maintaining a reserve ratio of 10 percent, the loan amounts to €72.900. The balance sheet of C is as follows:

Debit		Credit	
Cash	€81.000	Deposit from X	€81.000
Loan to person Y	€72.900	Deposit of person Y	€72.900

We could now continue the process of money creation further. Under the assumption of no friction or unused loans and a reserve ratio of 10 percent, the banking system can multiply by 10 the originary deposited €100.000.[2]

In a miraculous way, the banking system has created new money in form of bank accounts. Now, the money supply is €1.000.000. The BMW dealer, person V, X, etc. hold together €1.000.000 in their bank accounts. The banking system holds a cash reserve of ten percent (€100.000). The very profitable business of creating money has only become possible because of the privilege of the government, which in our experiment is *you*. In some sense, the government is the boss of the banking system and person Y might be the government itself. You gave the banks the privilege of creating money and in exchange, banks finance you by granting you loans or buying bonds issued by you. In fact, when we put aside all of the distracting manoeuvres and intricacies, it is easier to think of the owner of the printing press, you (the government) and the banking system as one institution. The franchise system of fractional reserve banking potentiates the power of the money creation.

---

[2] Find below a more complete table showing the credit expansion in a system of small banks after Huerta de Soto, *Money, Bank Credit, and Economic Cycles*, p. 230.

	Money remaining in each bank's vault	Credit expansion (Loans created ex nihilo)	Deposits
Bank A	10.000	90.000	100.000
Bank B	9.000	81.000	90.000
Bank C	8.100	72.900	81.000
Bank D	7.290	65.600	72.900
Bank E	6.560	59.000	65.600
Bank F	5.970	53.100	59.000
Bank G	5.310	47.800	53.100
Bank H	4.780	43.000	47.800
Bank I	4.300	38.700	43.000
Bank J	3.780	34.000	37.800
. .	.	.	.

Banking system			
Total	d=100.000	x= d(1-c)/c= 900.000	d/c= 1.000.000

[d = originary deposits; x = money created by credit expansion; c = reserve ratio]
Note: The last three digits have been rounded.

Out of €100.000 newly printed notes, the system made €1.000.000. By buying your bonds, bond prices are bid up and yields fall. You enjoy lower interest rates.

The connections between central bankers, bankers, and the government are not superficial. They form an elite group that cooperates closely. Bankers and politicians are seldom critical of each other. They frequently dine and chat with each other. The government establishes its own printing press (central bank). The central bank buys, to a large extent, government bonds, financing the government. The government pays interest on these bonds which increase the central bank profits. These central bank profits are then remitted to the government. When the bonds come due, the government does not have to pay the principal either, because the central bank buys a new bond that serves to pay the old one; the debt is rolled-over. On a lower level, the franchise system comes into play. Banks have the privilege of creating money. Banks also buy government bonds, or use them as collateral to obtain loans from the central bank. Banks do not only finance the government with the new money; an important part of their business is to give loans to consumers and entrepreneurs. Nevertheless, the banking system never betrays the government and finances its debts. It is rewarded by the central bank that buys government bonds from the banking system outright, or accepts them as collateral for new loans to the banking system.

At the end of the day, the system is simple. A printing press produces huge temptations: being able to buy votes or fulfil political dreams, for example. By using the printing press, the redistribution favors the government and the first receivers of the new money—to the detriment of the rest. This scheme is providently concealed by the government by separating the money flows institutionally. The central bank is made "independent" but still buys government bonds and remits profits back to the government. Banks, in a franchise system, participate in the advantages of money production and in turn help to finance the government. While the connections are complicated, it boils down to nothing more than one individual having a printing press and using it for his own benefit.

CHAPTER SEVEN

Differences in the Money Creation of the Fed and the ECB

Both the Fed and the ECB engage in the profitable business of monopolistic paper money production. They own the printing presses to produce dollars and Euros respectively. But in terms of its mission, the Fed is inherently more inflationary due to its dualistic tradition and mandate: to ensure price stability and growth on an equal footing. The ECB, in contrast, has a hierarchical objective: Achieve price stability first, and then support economic policies.[1]

When it comes to operational policies, there exist only slight differences between the two central banks. The Federal Reserve (Fed) has traditionally bought and sold government bonds in order to influence the money supply and the interest rate. Look at a simplified Federal Reserve balance sheet.

Debit		Credit	
Government bonds	$50	Notes	$20
Gold	$30	Bank reserves	$80
F/x reserves	$20		

---

[1] A good comparison of the ECB and the Fed that also includes a breakdown of their organization can be found in Stephen G. Cecchetti and Róisín O'Sullivan, "The European Central Bank and the Federal Reserve," *Oxford Review of Economic Policy* 19 (1, 2003): pp. 30–43.

In this example the Federal Reserve has supplied a monetary base of one hundred dollars, consisting of twenty dollars in circulating bank notes and eighty dollars in form of deposits that banks hold at the Fed. Against these liabilities the Fed holds as assets fifty dollars in government bonds, thirty dollars in gold, and twenty dollars in foreign exchange reserves. On top of these reserves and notes, the fractional reserve banking system can expand the money supply by granting more loans or buying government bonds.

If the Fed wants to add bank reserves to the system it usually buys government bonds. Let us imagine that the Fed buys fifty dollars worth of government bonds from the banking system.

Debit		Credit	
Government bonds	$100	Notes	$20
Gold	$30	Bank reserves	$130
F/x reserves	$20		

This implies an increase in government bonds to $100 on the asset side and of bank reserves to $130 on the liability side. The purchase of government bonds is called an *open market operation*. The Fed usually uses open market operations once a week to manipulate the federal fund rate, i.e., the interest rate for lending bank reserves overnight in the interbank market. When bank reserves increase, the federal fund rate tends to fall and vice versa. The focus on the federal funds target rate directs attention away from the underlying scheme, i.e., increases in the money supply in favor of the government and its friends. The initiative for changing the supply of base money is on part of the Fed.

Another way of increasing bank reserves is through lending to banks. This can be done, as in the case of the Fed, in the form of repurchase agreements (repos)—on the debit side of the balance sheet repurchase agreements increase, on the credit side bank reserves increase. In a repo, the borrower agrees to sell a security to a lender and agrees to buy it back in the future at a fixed price.

The price difference is the interest paid. Fed repos are also a form of open market operation. They are done on a daily basis and have usually been of very short maturity (overnight).

In order to borrow through repos from the Fed, banks need to provide an underlying security, also called collateral. The collateral is like a guarantee for the Fed. If the bank cannot pay back the loan, the Fed still has the collateral to recover funds. The Fed has traditionally accepted US government bonds as an underlying asset in repurchase agreements. The Fed makes sure that there is a constant demand for government bonds; banks know they are accepted as collateral for loans. The scheme plays out like this: equipped with their privilege of holding only fractional reserves, banks create money out of thin air. With a part of the newly created money they purchase government bonds—because the Fed accepts these bonds as collateral or may buy them outright. As a consequence of the purchase of government bonds by the banking system, bond yields decrease. The government pays lower interest rates on its debts as a result.

Another form of lending is done through the so-called "discount window." Here the initiative is on the part of banks. They may borrow overnight money through the discount window at an interest rate that is higher than the federal fund target rate. The discount window is an instrument for banks that are in need of funds and willing to pay a higher interest rate. In normal times, the discount window is not used by banks due to the penalty rate. And who uses the discount window is a matter of public knowledge, making it an unattractive alternative.

During the crisis of 2008, the Fed started other lending programmes with longer maturities that were directed at a broader range of entities (not only commercial banks) and accepted a broader range of collateral. The Fed also started to buy considerable amounts of agency debt and mortgage backed securities issued by Freddie Mac and Fannie Mae.

The ECB operates similarly to the Fed, while offering some peculiarities. The ECB uses three main instruments for its monetary policy (euphemism for money production): changes in minimum reserves, open market operations, and standing facilities. Banks must hold reserves in their accounts at the ECB based on their deposits. For €100 deposited by a customer, a bank must keep €2 at its account at the ECB; the bank may lend €98. By reducing (or increasing) the required minimum reserves banks must hold in their accounts at the ECB, banks may expand credits (or are forced to contract credits). However, this instrument is normally not touched and required reserves for demand deposits are held constant at two percent.

More relevant are open market operations and standing facilities (the marginal lending facility and the deposit facility). The difference between the two is that the initiative of open market operations is on the part of the ECB, while the initiative of standby facilities is on the part of the banks. Through the deposit facility, banks can deposit money overnight at the ECB, receiving interest. The rate of the deposit facility is the lower limit for interbank rates. No bank would accept a lower rate for funds in the interbank market because it can get the deposit facility rate at the ECB. In the marginal lending facility (similar to the discount window of the Fed), banks can borrow money from the ECB at penalty rates. Through the marginal lending facility, the ECB creates new base money only if it is asked for by banks. The marginal lending rate represents the upper limit for the interbank rate, as no bank would pay a higher rate than the one it pays for in the marginal lending facility.

The marginal lending facility comes with two further requirements for banks. First, banks may get money at the penalty rate through the marginal lending facility only if they provide sufficient collateral. The collateral has to be of certain quality. The quality is certified by three licensed, i.e., privileged rating agencies: Moody's, Fitch, and Standard and Poor's. If a bond is rated as risky and of low quality, the ECB will not accept it as collateral for its loans.

Second, a haircut (deduction from securities value) is applied in relation to the maturity and risk of the security (collateral). If a bank offers a bond worth €1000 as collateral, it will not be able to obtain a loan worth €1000, but a lower amount. The haircut serves as protection against potential losses. Imagine that the bank cannot pay back its loan and the ECB has to sell the bond to recover funds. In the meantime the value of the bond has fallen to €900. If no haircut had been applied, the ECB would suffer losses of €100. Losses are in principle not a problem for the ECB because it does not depend on the profit and loss motive. The ECB could continue to operate, since it can always just create money to pay its bills and lend to the banking system. However, central banks try to avoid losses as they reduce their equity. Losses might require strange accounting moves and reduce confidence in a currency. If the haircut is ten percent, the bank may get a loan of €900 against the bond of €1000. Unsurprisingly, haircuts for government bonds are lower than for other types of securities. This is another way of discretely favoring government finance with new money creation.

In contrast to the marginal lending facility, the initiative in open market operations is on the part of the ECB. There are basically two main ways to produce money through open market operations. First, the ECB purchases or sells securities outright. The outright purchase or sale is not the normal procedure for manipulating the money supply.

Normally, the ECB uses the second method and lends new money to banks via its lending facilities, which differ in purpose and term. There is the structural refinancing facility, the fine tuning facility (Does the term remind you of *social engineering*?), the long term refinancing facility and the main refinancing facility. In these facilities, securities are not purchased but used in reversed transactions: repos or collateralized loans. A collateralized loan is similar to a repo.

In a repo, the ECB buys a security with new money and sells it back at a higher price, the difference being the interest rate. It may buy a security at €1000 and sell it at €1010 in one year, implying an interest rate of one percent.

In a collateralized loan, however, the bank receives a loan of €1000, pledging the security as collateral and paying €10 interest. The difference between the repo and the collateralized loan is basically legal in nature. In the repo, the ownership of the collateral changes to the ECB, while in the collateralized loan, ownership stays with the borrowing bank that pledges it as collateral.

Week for week the ECB decides how much base money it wants to inject in the EMU. Maturities are normally of two weeks. The ECB basically auctions the money off via fixed or variable rate tender. In the fixed tender the interest rate is fixed by the ECB and the banks receive new money pro rata for their bids. In the variable rate tender, the banks bid for an amount of money and offer an interest rate. They are served in relation to their interest bids.

DIFFERENCES

One of the main differences between the ECB and the Fed is that the ECB has always accepted a broader range of collateral, making its policies more "flexible." The Fed accepts or buys in its open market operations only AAA rated securities, namely treasuries, federal agency debt, or mortgage debt securities guaranteed by federal agencies.[2] In the discount window, investment grade securities are accepted (rated BBB– and higher).[3]

The ECB has traditionally accepted a broader range of collateral in its open market operations. Beside government bonds, the ECB also accepts mortgage backed securities, covered bank loans, and other debt instruments that are at least rated with A–. This minimum rating was reduced as an emergency measure during the crisis to BBB–, and with the plan that it would expire after one year. Before the exception could expire, however, the measure was extended because Greece's rating was in danger of falling too low. Finally, the exception was made for Greek bonds, which would be accepted irrespective of their rating.

Both central banks support government debt, but in different ways. While the Fed uses only government bonds or agency debt or securities guaranteed by agencies, fostering their demand, the

---

[2] See Federal Reserve, "The Federal Reserve System: Purposes and Functions," 9th ed. (2005), http://www.federalreserve.gov, pp. 39–40.

[3] Ibid., p. 50.

ECB brings forward a bias for government debts by applying a lower haircut.

Another small difference between the Fed and the ECB lies in the way the money supply is altered, i.e., the way they produce new money. In their open market operations, the Fed prefers outright purchases of securities, whereas the ECB prefers reverse transactions.

Imagine that the Fed wants to increase bank reserves by $1000. It buys an additional $1000 worth of government bonds. Bank reserves are increased by $1000 as long as the Fed does not sell the bonds back to the banking system. The Fed receives the interest rates paid on the government bonds, remitting them back to the government in form of profit.

If the ECB has the aim of increasing the money supply by €1000, it auctions an additional €1000 in reverse transactions, accepting government bonds as collateral and applying haircuts. The ECB also receives interest payments on the loan. It remits these interest payments in form of profit to its member banks that send them along to their respective governments. When the loans come due, the ECB can roll-over the loan. In this case, the increase in bank reserves of €1000 is maintained. Government bonds are used de facto to create new money in both cases. The operation is undone when the Fed sells the government bond or when the ECB fails to roll over the loan to the banking system.

HOW THE ECB FINANCES GOVERNMENTS

When governments spend more than they receive in taxes, they issue bonds. In contrast to the FED, the ECB[4] normally does not buy these bonds outright (this changed with the recent sovereign debt crisis).[5] Imagine a bond worth €1000 with a

---

[4] It would be more precise to state "Eurosystem" instead of "ECB." The Eurosystem consists of the central banks of the member states plus the ECB. However, as the central banks of the member states only carry out the orders of the ECB within their respective countries, we usually simplify by using the term "ECB."

[5] See Rita Nazareth and Gavin Serkin, "Stocks, Commodities, Greek Bonds Rally on European Loan Package," *Bloomberg* (May 10, 2010), http://noir. bloomberg.com.

maturity of 10 years is sold by a government. Banks will buy the bond, possibly by creating new money, because they know the ECB will accept the bond as collateral.

The ECB accepts the bond in a reverse transaction such as a collateralized loan with a maturity of one week (or one month), lending new money to the banks. After the week is up, the ECB will just renew the loan and accept the bond if it wants to maintain the money supply. The ECB may continue to do so for ten years. After ten years, the government will have to pay back the bond and will probably do so by issuing another bond, and so on. The government never has to pay its debt; it just issues new debt to pay the old one. But does the government at least pay the interest payments on the bond? The interest payments are paid to the ECB. As mentioned before, part of the interest payment flows back to the government as ECB profits are remitted according to the capital of the different national central banks. From there profits flow to the respective governments. What about the interest payments that aren't flowing back, i.e., remitted back to the government in the form of profits? Don't governments have to pay for those? Again, the government may just issue a new bond to pay for these expenditures. The banks buy the bond and the ECB accepts it as collateral. In this way, the ECB is able to finance the deficits of member states.

How is it possible, then, that Greece ran into refinancing problems? Greece had problems rolling over its debt. It was feared that the ECB would not accept Greek bonds anymore, and that the rating would fall below the minimum. Moreover, many market participants began to speculate that political problems caused by rising deficits and debts could end the monetization of Greek debts. At some point the German or other European governments would step in and demand that the ECB stop financing Greece's growing debts and deficits. It was also feared that other countries would not bail Greece out with direct government loans. This kind of direct support runs counter to terms of the Treaty of Maastricht, not to mention the severe political difficulties that come along with trying to persuade the population.

Greece's rescue, in the end, may not have been economically viable. The danger of default rose and interest rates for Greek bonds soared, leading to the sovereign debt crises.

CHARTER EIGHT
———————

The EMU as a Self-Destroying System

When property rights in money are poorly defined, negative external effects develop. The institutional setup of the Euro, with its poorly defined property rights, has brought it close to collapse and can be called a tragedy of the commons.[1]

FIAT MONEY AND EXTERNAL COSTS

External costs and benefits are the result of ill-defined or defended property rights.[2] The proprietor does not assume the

———————

[1] I have developed this argument in an academic paper published in *The Independent Review* [Philipp Bagus, "The Tragedy of the Euro," *The Independent Review* 15 (4, 2011)]. The present chapter draws on this paper and extends the explanation.

[2] Ludwig von Mises, *Human Action,* Scholar's Edition (Auburn, Ala.: Ludwig von Mises Institute, 1998), p. 651. We have to emphasize that we are referring here to positive or negative consequences resulting from ill-defined or ill-defended property rights. We are not referring to psychological or monetary consequences of actions. Keeping flowers in the garden can have positive or negative effects on the welfare of the neighbor. The effects on the welfare of the neighbor are usually called psychological external effects. In the literature there is also another external effect. If a movie theatre is build next to a restaurant there will probably be positive monetary effects for the restaurant owner in that customers will attend the restaurant because of the theatre. There may also be negative external effects on alternative restaurants. These effects are usually called pecuniary external effects. When we talk in this chapter about external effects we are concerned neither with

full advantages or disadvantages of employing a property. As the actor is not fully responsible for the effects of his actions, he will not take into account all the consequences of his actions.

The actor that does not reap some of the benefits of his actions will not take into account all the positive effects of it. An example of these positive (external) benefits might be an apple tree owner whose property rights over the apples growing on the tree are not secured. People walking down the street just grab any apples within their reach. This behavior is permitted by the government. The apple tree owner would probably neglect the tree or even cut the tree down to burn the wood. Yet, he would act differently were he the sole benefactor of the tree. He would protect the tree against insects and troublemakers.

Similarly, the proprietor may incur some external costs. External costs result from the absence of property rights. External costs do not burden the proprietor, but others. The proprietor will engage in some projects he would not have if he had had to assume all costs. An example of external costs would be the owner of a factory that dumps its waste into a public lake. This lake may be privately owned by a third party, but the government does not defend the property rights of the lake's owner because it regards the factory as essential for economic growth. In this scenario the factory owner does not have to assume the full cost of production, but can externalize some part of the costs to others by dumping the waste. If the factory owner had to pay for its disposal, however, he would probably act differently. He might produce less, or operate in a more waste-preventing way. Since the property rights of the lake are not well defended or not defined at all (in the case of public property in the lake), the factory owner is released from the responsibility of some of the costs incurred. As a consequence, there is more pollution than would be seen otherwise.

---

psychological nor monetary effects of actions. All actions may have these effects. Rather we are concerned with the effects of actions resulting from ill-defined or ill-defended property. In terms of the orthodox literature we deal with technological externalities rather than pecuniary or psychological ones.

In our present monetary system there are several levels on which property rights are not clearly defined and defended. At a first level, private property rights are absent in the field of base money production. The private money, gold, was nationalized during the twentieth century. And private money production of commodity moneys belongs to the past.

It is important to point out that under the gold standard there were no external (technological) effects involved in base money production. Private gold producers incurred substantial costs mining the gold and they reaped the full benefits. It is true that the increase in the gold money supply tended to push up prices and, therefore, involved pecuniary external effects. But an increase in the production of goods affecting the purchasing power of money and relative prices does not imply any private property violation. Anyone was free to search for and mine gold and could sell it on the market. No one was forced to accept the gold in payment. Moreover, private property in base money production was defended.

The loss in purchasing power caused by mining brought along redistributive effects. Redistributive effects alone, however, do not imply external effects. Any change in market data has redistributive effects. If the production of apples increases, their price falls, benefiting some people, especially those who like apples. If there is a free market increase of gold money or apples, there are redistribution, but no bad application of private property rights and, consequently, no external (technological) costs.

Furthermore, the increase in gold money did not have the negative external effect of decreasing the quality of money.[3] By increasing the number of gold coins, the average metal content of a gold coin was not reduced. Gold could continue to fulfil its purposes as a medium of exchange and a store of value.

During the twentieth century, governments absorbed and monopolized the production of money. Private gold money with clearly defined property rights was replaced by public fiat money.

---

[3] For the quality of money see Philipp Bagus, "The Quality of Money," *Quarterly Journal of Austrian Economics* 12 (4, 2009): pp. 41–64.

This money monopoly itself implies a violation of property rights. Central banks alone could produce base money, i.e., notes or reserves at the central bank. Property rights are also infringed upon because fiat money is legal tender. Everyone has to accept it for debt payments and the government accepts only the legal tender fiat money for tax payments.[4]

By giving fiat money a privileged position and by mono-polising its production, property rights in money are not defended and the costs of money production are partially forced upon other actors. If no one had to accept public paper money and everyone could produce it, no external costs would evolve. People could simply decide not to accept fiat money or produce it themselves.

The benefits of the production of money fall to its producer, i.e., central banks and their controller (governments). External costs in the form of rising prices and, in most cases, a lower quality of money, are imposed on all users of fiat money. Not only do additional monetary units tend to bid up prices, but the quality of money tends to fall as well. The average quality of assets backing the currency is normally reduced by fiat money production.

Imagine that twenty percent of the monetary base is backed by gold reserves. If the central bank buys government bonds, mortgage-backed securities, or increases bank lending and increases the supply of fiat base money by one hundred percent, the average quality of base money falls. After these expansionary policies, only ten percent of base money is backed by gold and ninety percent is backed by assets of a lower quality.

The gold reserve ratio is even relevant if there is no redemption promise. Gold reserves can prop up confidence in a currency and can be used in panic situations to defend the currency. They are also important to have in the case of monetary reforms. In contrast to the fiat paper situation, where an increase in money

---

[4] For a description of government interventions into the monetary system and a reform proposal see Hans Sennholz, *Money and Freedom* (Spring Mills, Pa.: Libertarian Press, 1985).

supply dilutes the quality of the currency, there is no dilution in the quality of the currency by gold mining. By minting new coins, the quality of previously existing gold coins is untouched.

Due to the infringement on private property rights in base money production, governments can profit from base money production and externalize some costs. The benefits for governments are clear. They may finance their expenditure with the new money through the detour of the central bank. Costs are shifted onto the population in the form of a lower quality of money and a lower purchasing power of money.

THE TRAGEDY OF THE COMMONS AND BANKING

Another layer in the monetary system of ill-defined property rights is the tragedy of the commons in banking. A "tragedy of the commons," a term coined by Garrett Hardin,[5] is a special case of the external costs problem. As explained above, external costs generally occur when property rights are not well defined or defended, and when a single privileged owner can externalize costs on others. This is the case of the factory owner being allowed to dump waste in the private lake or the case of the central bank producing legal tender base money supported by the state. In a tragedy of the commons, a specific characteristic is added to the external cost problem. Not one but several actors exploiting one property can externalize costs on others. Not only one factory owner, but many can dump waste into the private lake. Likewise, more than one bank can produce fiduciary media.

The traditional examples for a tragedy of the commons are common properties such as public beaches or schools of fish in the ocean. They are exploited without regard to the disadvantages that can be partially externalized. Benefits are obtained by numerous users, but some of the costs are externalized. Let us look at the incentives for a single fisherman. By fishing the

---

[5] Garrett Hardin, "The Tragedy of the Commons," *Science* New Series 162 (3859, 1968): pp. 1243–1248.

school, the fisherman obtains the benefits in the form of the fish; however, the cost of a reduced size of the school is borne by all.

If there were private property rights that defined the school, the school's owner would fully assume the costs of reducing its size. The owner would have an interest in its long-term preservation. He would not only own the present use (hunted fish) but also the capital value of the school. The owner knows that every fish he catches may reduce the number of fish for the future. He balances the costs and benefits of fishing and decides consequently on the number of fish he wants to catch. He has an interest in the capital value or long term preservation of the school.

The situation changes radically when the school is public property. There is an incentive to overfish (i.e., overexploit) the resource because the benefits are internalized and the costs are partially externalized. All benefits go to the fisherman, whereas the damage suffered through the reduction of the school is shared by the whole group. In fact, there is the incentive to fish as fast as possible, given the knowledge of the incentives for other fishermen. If I do not fish, another will fish and get the benefits, whereas I bear the costs of the reduced size of the school. In a "pure" tragedy of the commons, there are no limits to overexploitation, and the resource disappears as a result.

The concept of the tragedy of the commons can be applied successfully to other areas such as the political system. Hans-Hermann Hoppe[6] applied the concept to democracy. In a democracy there is public entrance into government. In government one gains access to the property of the whole country by using the coercive apparatus of the state. Benefits of appropriation of private property are internalized by the government while costs are borne by the whole population. After one term, other people may gain access to the coercive apparatus. Thus, the incentive is to exploit the privilege in its limits as much as possible while in power.

---

[6] Hans-Hermann Hoppe, *Democracy: The God that Failed* (Rutgers, NJ: Transaction Publishers, 2001).

Another fruitful application of the tragedy of the commons is in the monetary field. In our modern banking system,[7] where property rights are not clearly defined and defended,[8] any bank can produce fiduciary media, i.e., unbacked demand deposits, by expanding credits. At the level of base money, when a single central bank can produce money, there is no tragedy of the commons. Yet, at the level of the banking system, a tragedy of the commons occurs precisely because any bank can produce fiduciary media.

In banking, traditional legal principles of deposit contracts are not respected.[9] It is not clear if bank customers actually lend money to banks or if they make genuine deposits. Genuine deposits require the full availability of the money to the depositor. In fact, full availability may be the reason why most people hold demand deposits. Yet, banks have been granted the legal privilege to use the money deposited to them. As such, property rights in the deposited money are unclear.

Banks that make use of their legal privilege and the unclear definition of private property rights in deposits can make very large profits. They can create deposits out of nothing and grant loans to earn interest. The temptation to expand credit is almost irresistible. Moreover, banks will try to expand credit and issue fiduciary media as much and as fast as they can. This credit expansion entails the typical feature found in the tragedy of the commons—external costs. In this case, everyone in society is

---

[7] Huerta de Soto, *Money, Bank Credit and Economic Cycles*, p. 666.

[8] George A. Selgin and Lawrence H. White, "In Defense of Fiduciary Media, or We are Not (Devo)lutionists, We are Misesians!" *Review of Austrian Economics* 9 (2, 1996), fn. 12, do not distinguish between pecuniary and technological external effects. They do not see any property rights violation in the issuance of fiduciary media or any difference between issuing fiduciary media and gold mining in a gold standard. Yet, there are important differences. Both affect the price level, but one violates private property rights and the other does not. Huerta de Soto, *Money, Bank Credit and Economic Cycles*, and Hans-Hermann Hoppe, Jörg Guido Hülsmann and Walter Block, "Against Fiduciary Media," *Quarterly Journal of Austrian Economics* 1 (1, 1998): pp. 19–50, pointed to the important differences of changes in prices caused by increases in money supply with and without property rights violations.

[9] Huerta de Soto, *Money, Bank Credit and Economic Cycles*.

harmed by the price changes induced by the issue of fiduciary media.

There are, however, several differences between a fractional reserve banking system and a tragedy of the commons (like a public fish school). In Hardin's analysis, there is virtually no limit to the exploitation of the "unowned" properties that have no clearly defined ownership. Further exploitation of the public resource stops only when the costs become higher than the benefits, i.e., when the school is so small that searching for the remaining fish is no longer worthwhile. Likewise for the fractional reserve banks on the free market, there are important limits on the issuing of fiduciary media at the expense of clients. This limit is set by the behavior of the other banks and their clients in a free banking system. More specifically, credit expansion is limited since banks, via the clearing system, can force each other into bankruptcy.

Let's assume there are two banks: bank A and bank B. Bank A expands credit while bank B does not. Money titles issued by bank A are exchanged between clients of bank A and clients of bank B. At some point, the clients of bank B or bank B will demand redemption for the money titles from bank A. Hence, bank A will lose some of its reserves, for instance, gold. As is every fractional reserve bank, bank A is inherently bankrupt; it cannot redeem all the money titles it has issued. If bank B and its clients demand that bank A redeem the money titles to a degree that it cannot fulfil, bank A must declare bankruptcy.

The clearing system and the clients of other banks demanding redemption set narrow limits on the issuing of fiduciary media. Banks have a certain incentive to restrict expansion of fiduciary media to a greater extent than their rival banks, with the final aim being to force their competitors into bankruptcy. In other words, these banks naturally want to exploit the great profit opportunities offered by the improperly defined property rights, but they can only expand credit to the extent that the risk of bankruptcy is reasonably avoided. Competition forces them to check their credit expansion.

The question now concerns how the banks can increase the profits from credit expansion while keeping the risk of bankruptcy low. The solution, obviously, is to form agreements with each other in order to avoid the negative consequences of an independent and uncoordinated credit expansion. As a result, banks set a common policy of simultaneous credit expansion. These policies permit them to remain solvent, to maintain their reserves in relation to one another, and to make huge profits.

Therefore, the tragedy of the commons not only predicts the exploitation and external costs of vaguely defined private property, it also explains why there is pressure in a free-banking system to form agreements, mergers, and cartels. However, even with the forming of cartels, the threat of bankruptcy remains. In other words, the incentive to force competitors into bankruptcy still remains, resulting in the instability of the cartels.

For fractional reserve banks, there is a great demand for the introduction of a central bank that coordinates the credit expansion of the banking system. The one difference between the tragedy of the commons applied to the environment and the tragedy of the commons applied to a free banking system— limits on exploitation—is now removed by the introduction of the central bank. Hence, according to Huerta de Soto, a true "tragedy of the commons" situation occurs only when a central bank is installed. The banks can now exploit the improperly defined property without restriction.

Even in the most comfortable scenario for the banks, i.e., the installation of a central bank and fiat money, there remain other limits. The central bank may try to regulate bank lending and thereby control and limit credit expansion to some extent. The ultimate check on credit expansion, the risk of hyperinflation, remains also. In other words, even with the creation of a central bank, there is still a check on the exploitation of private property. In an ideal "tragedy of the commons" situation, the drive is to exploit ill-defined property as quickly as possible and forestall exploitation of other agents. But even with the existence of a central bank that guarantees their liquidity, it is not in the interest of the fractional reserve banks to issue fiduciary media as quickly as possible. To do so could lead to a runaway hyperinflation. The exploitation of the commons must therefore be stretched and implemented carefully.

The overexploitation of public property can be restricted in several ways. The simplest way is a privatization of the public property. Private property rights are finally defined and defended. Another solution is the moral persuasion and education of the actors that exploit the commons. For instance, fishermen can voluntarily restrict the exploitation of the school. A further option is the regulation of the commons to restrict the overexploitation of the commons. Hardin[10] calls these regulated commons "managed commons." Government limits the exploitation.

An example is the introduction of fishing quotas that provide every fisherman a certain quota per year. Each receives a monopoly right that he will try to exploit fully. Overexploitation is, thus, reduced and managed. In the case of today's banking system, we have a managed commons. Central banks and banking regulation coordinate and limit the credit expansion of banks. By requiring minimum reserves and managing the amount of bank reserves as well as the interest rates, central banks can limit credit expansion and the external costs of the reduced purchasing power of money.

THE EURO AND THE TRAGEDY OF THE COMMONS

Although the external effects of a monopolistic money producer and a fractional reserve banking system regulated by a central bank are common in the Western world, the establishment of the Euro implies a third and unique layer of external effects. The institutional setup of the Eurosystem in the EMU is such that all governments can use the ECB to finance their deficits.

A central bank can finance the deficits of a single government by buying government bonds or accepting them as collateral for new loans to the banking system resulting. Now we are faced

---

[10] Hardin, "The Tragedy of the Commons."

with a situation in which several governments are able to finance themselves via a single central bank: the ECB.

When governments in the EMU run deficits, they issue bonds. A substantial part of these bonds are bought by the banking system.[11] The banking system is happy to buy these bonds because they are accepted as preferred collateral in the lending operations of the ECB.[12] Furthermore, banks are required by regulation to hold a certain proportion of their funds in "High Quality Liquid Assets" which encourages them to invest in government securities. This means that it is essential and profitable for banks to own government bonds. By presenting the bonds as collateral, banks can receive new money from the ECB.

The mechanism work as follows: banks create new money by credit expansion. They exchange the money against government bonds and use them to refinance with the ECB. The end result is that the governments finance their deficits with new money created by banks, and the banks receive new base money by pledging the bonds as collateral.[13]

---

[11] It is hard to say how much European government debt is held by European banks. It may be around thirty percent. The rest is held by insurances, monetary funds, investment funds, and foreign governments and banks. The private sector institutions investing in government bonds do so in part because banks provide a steady demand for this valuable collateral. Unfortunately, we do not know either how much of the government bond issue ends up with the Eurosystem as collateral because the information on the collateral is not published by the ECB.

[12] See ECB, *The Implementation of Monetary Policy in the Euro Area: General Documentation on Eurosystem Monetary Policy Instruments and Procedures* (November, 2008), available at http://www.ecb.int, for the operation of the EMU and the collateral rules of the ECB.

[13] In addition to the outright monetization of government bonds there is an indirect monetization occurring within the financial system. Market participants know that central banks buy government bonds and accept them as the preferred collateral. Thus, banks buy the bonds due to their privileged treatment ensuring a liquid market and pushing down yields. On another level, knowing that there is a very liquid market in government bonds and a high demand by banks, investment funds, pension funds, insurers and private investors buy government bonds. Government bonds become very liquid and almost as good as base money. In many cases they serve to create additional base money. In other cases they stand as a reserve to be converted

The incentive is clear: redistribution. First users of the new money benefit. Governments and banks have more money available; they profit because they can still buy at prices that have not yet been bid up by the new money. When governments start spending the money, prices are bid up. Monetary incomes increase. The higher the deficits become and the more governments issue bonds, the more prices and incomes rise. When prices and incomes increase in the deficit country, the new money starts to flow abroad where the effect on prices is not yet felt. Goods and services are bought and imported from other EMU countries where prices have not yet risen. The new money spreads through the whole monetary union.

In the EMU, the deficit countries that use the new money first win. Naturally, there is also a losing side in this monetary redistribution. Deficit countries benefit at the cost of the later receivers of the new money. The later receivers are mainly in foreign member states that do not run such high deficits. The later receivers lose as their incomes start to rise only after prices increase. They see their real income reduced. In the EMU, the benefits of the increase in the money supply go to the first users, whereas the damage to the purchasing power of the monetary unit is shared by all users of the currency. Not only does the purchasing power of money in the EU fall due to excessive deficits, but interest rates tend to increase due to the excessive demand coming from over-indebted governments. Countries that are more fiscally responsible have to pay higher interest

---

into base money if necessary. As a consequence, new money created through credit expansion often ends up buying liquid government bonds, indirectly monetising the debt. Imagine that the government has a deficit and issues government bonds. A part of it is bought by the banking system and used to get additional reserves from the central bank who buys the bonds or grants new loans, accepting them as collateral. The banking system uses the new reserves to expand credits and grant loans to, for example, the construction industry. With the new loans the construction industry buys factors of production and pays its workers. The workers use part of the new money to invest in investment funds. The investment funds then use the new money to acquire government bonds. Thus, there is an indirect monetization. Part of the money created by the fractional reserve banking system ends up buying government bonds because of their preferential treatment by the central bank, i.e. its outright monetization.

rates on their debts due to the extravagance of others. The consequence is a tragedy of the commons. Any government running deficits can profit at the cost of other governments with more balanced budgetary policies.[14]

Imagine, for example, that several individuals possess a printing press for the same fiat currency. These individuals have the incentive to print money and spend it, bidding up prices. The benefits in the form of a higher income accrue to the owners of the printing press, whereas the costs of the action in the form of a lower purchasing power of money are borne by all users of the currency. The consequent incentive is to print money as fast as possible. A printing press owner who does not engage in printing will see prices rise. Other owners will use the press in order to benefit from the loss in purchasing power that affects other printing press owners. The owner who prints the fastest makes gains at the expense of the slower printing owners. We are faced with a "pure" tragedy of the commons. There is no limit to the exploitation of the resource.[15] As in the case of public natural resources, there is an overexploitation that ends with the destruction of the resource. In this case, the currency ends in a hyperinflation and a crack-up boom.

Although the example of several press owners printing the same currency helps us understand the situation in a visual way, it does not apply exactly to the EMU. But differences between the two setups help explain why there is no pure tragedy of the commons in the Eurosystem and why the Euro has not yet disappeared. The most obvious difference is that deficit countries cannot print Euros directly. Governments can only issue their

---

[14] An additional moral hazard problem arises when banks holding government debts are bailed out through monetary expansion. Banks knowing that they will be bailed out and their government debts will be bought by the central bank will behave more recklessly and continue to finance irresponsible governments.

[15] On the incentives to convert public property into "pure" tragedies of the commons and eliminate limits on its exploitation see Philipp Bagus, "La tragedia de los bienes comunales y la escuela austriaca: Hardin, Hoppe, Huerta de Soto y Mises," *Procesos de Mercado: Revista Europea de Economía Política* 1 (2, 2004): pp. 125–134.

own bonds. There is no guarantee that banks will buy these bonds and use them as collateral for new loans from the ECB.

In reality, there are several reasons why the scheme might not work.

1. Banks may not buy government bonds and use them as collateral if the operation is not attractive. The interest rate offered for the government bonds might not be high enough in comparison with the interest rates they pay for loans from the ECB. Governments must then offer higher yields to attract banks as buyers.

2. The default risk on the government bonds might deter banks. In the EMU this default risk has been reduced by implicit bailout guarantees from the beginning. It was understood that once a country introduced the Euro, it would never leave the EMU. The Euro is quite correctly seen as a political project and a step toward political integration. Jacques Delors put it bluntly in February 1995: "EMU means, for instance, that the Union acknowledges the debt of all those countries that are in the EMU."[16]

The default of a member state and a resulting exit would not only be seen as a failure of the Euro, but also as a failure of the socialist version of the European Union. Politically, a default is seen as next to impossible. Most believe that, in the worst case, stronger member states would support the weaker ones. Before it came to a default, countries such as Germany would guarantee the bonds of Mediterranean nations. The guarantees reduced the default risk of government loans from member states considerably.

Implicit guarantees have now become explicit. Greece was granted a rescue package of 110 billion Euros from the Eurozone and the International Monetary Fund (IMF).[17] In addition, 750 billion Euros have been pledged for further bailouts of other member states.[18]

---

[16] Quoted in Connolly, *The Rotten Heart of Europe*, p. 271fn.

[17] See Gabi Thesing and Flaiva Krause-Jackson, "Greece gets $146 Billion Rescue in EU, IMF Package," *Bloomberg* (May 3, 2010), http://noir.bloomberg.com.

[18] See Nazareth and Serkin, "Stocks, Commodities, Greek Bonds."

3. The ECB could decline to accept certain government bonds as collateral. The ECB requires a minimum rating for bonds to be accepted as collateral.[19] Before the financial crisis of 2008, the minimum rating was A–. During the financial crisis, it was reduced to BBB–. If ratings of bonds fall below the minimum rating, government bonds will not be accepted as collateral. This risk, however, is quite low. The ECB will probably not let a country fall in the future, and it has been accommodating in respect to the collateral rule in the past. The reduction of the minimum rating to BBB–was planned to expire after one year. When it became apparent that Greece would not maintain at least an A– rating, the rule was extended for another year. Finally, the ECB, in contrast to its stated principles of not applying special rules to a single country, announced it would accept Greek debt even if rated junk.[20]

4. The liquidity risk involved for banks using the ECB to refinance themselves by pledging government bonds as collateral may deter them. Government bonds are traditionally of a longer term than the loans granted by the ECB. There have traditionally been one-week and three-month loans in ECB lending operations. During the crisis, the maximum term was increased to one year. Nevertheless, most government bonds still have a longer term than ECB lending operations with maturities of up to 30 years. Consequently, the risk is that the rating of the bonds would be reduced over their lifetimes, and that the ECB might cease to accept them as collateral. In this scenario, the ECB would stop rolling over a loan collateralized by government bonds, causing liquidity problems for banks.

The risk of roll-over problems is relatively low; the ratings are supported by the implicit bailout guarantee and the political willingness to save the Euro project, as has been demonstrated by the sovereign debt crisis. Another side of the liquidity risk is that interest rates charged by the ECB might increase over time.

---

[19] More precisely, the ECB maintains a list of those securities which are eligible as collateral for the member central banks of the Eurosystem.

[20] See Marc Jones, "EU Will Accept Even Junk-rated Greek Bonds," *Reuters* (May 3, 2010), http://in.reuters.com.

Finally, they could be higher than the fixed rate of a longer term government bond. This risk is reduced by a sufficient interest spread between the yield of the government bond and the interest rates applied by the ECB. Moreover, the market value of the bond may fall over time. Should the market value of the bond become impaired, the associated loan must be partially redeemed or additional collateral must be provided.[21]

5. Haircuts applied by the ECB on the collateral do not allow for full refinancing. A bank offering 1,000,000 Euros worth of government bonds as collateral does not receive a loan of 1,000,000 Euros from the ECB, but a smaller amount. The reduction depends on the haircut applied to the collateral. The ECB distinguishes five different categories of collateral demanding different haircuts. Haircuts for government bonds are the smallest.[22] The ECB, thereby, subsidizes their use as collateral vis-à-vis other debt instruments supporting government borrowing.

6. The ECB might not accommodate all demands for new loans. Banks might offer more bonds as collateral than the ECB

---

[21] The market value and margin-call component of the collateral analysis for the Eurosystem is constrained by several factors. First, to maintain market values reasonably and updated promptly for all assets is a considerable task. Second, for many assets used as collateral (e.g. some mortgage backed securities) there is no deep market able to provide a reasonable liquid price. Third, for many assets the market price is at least partially determined by liquidity, which is in turn determined by the availability of funding from the Eurosystem so that the use of 'market pricing' is a circular exercise. Fourth, in the event of a severe deterioration in market conditions, and hence collateral value, it could well be that a margin call from the Eurosystem would be the final straw tipping a credit institution into insolvency – it is hard to see that the Eurosystem would be willing to accept the political consequences of such an action, and hence the practical value of the market value and margin mechanism is open to doubt. I would like to thank Robin Michaels for bringing this point to my attention.

[22] Haircuts often underestimate the risk of default as perceived by markets and are, therefore, artificially low. The Center for Geoeconomic Studies, "Greek Debt Crisis—Apocalypse Later," *Council on Foreign Relations* (September 2, 2010), http://blogs.cfr.org, used the difference between German and Greek government bonds yields to estimate the market's perception of the probability of a Greek default. This probability was eighty percent at the end of April 2010. Central government bonds with a residual of ten years only have a four to five percent haircut in the ECB's lending operations.

wants to supply in loans. Applying a restrictive monetary policy, not every bank offering government bonds as collateral will receive a loan. However, for political reasons, especially the will to continue the Euro project, one may expect that the ECB will accommodate such demands, especially if some governments are in trouble. Indeed, the ECB started offering unlimited liquidity to markets during the financial crisis. Any demand for a loan was satisfied — provided sufficient collateral was offered.

Even though we have not seen a pure tragedy of the commons in the Eurosystem, we have come close. With the current crisis, we are actually getting closer due to the ECB's direct buying of government bonds: the ECB announced the direct purchase of the bonds in May of 2010[23] to save the Euro project. If a government has deficits, it may issue bonds that are bought by banks and then by the ECB. Using this method, there is no longer a detour via the lending operations of the ECB. The ECB buys the bonds outright. The new development eliminates the majority of the aforementioned risks for the banking system.

The tragedy of the Euro is the incentive to incur higher deficits, issue government bonds, and make the whole Euro group burden the costs of irresponsible policies — in the form of the lower purchasing power of the Euro.[24] With such incentives, politicians tend to run high deficits. Why pay for higher expenditures by raising unpopular taxes? Why not just issue bonds that will be purchased by the creation of new money, even if it ultimately increases prices in the whole of the EMU? Why not externalize the costs of government spending?

The resulting moral hazard is asymmetrical. Governments of larger states would produce considerable inflationary pressure running high deficits and might be too big to be bailed out. On

---

[23] David Tweed and Simone Meier, "Trichet Indicates ECB Bond Purchases Not Unanimous," *Bloomberg* (May 10, 2010), http://noir.bloomberg.com.

[24] We are faced here with two sources of moral hazard. One arises from the working of the Eurosystem and the implicit bailout guarantee by the ECB, the other one from the implicit bailout guarantee by fellow governments. The effects are moral hazard and an excessive issue of government bonds.

the contrary, governments of smaller states would not produce much inflationary pressures even if they would run high deficits because the impact of the money creation would not be important for the Eurozone as a whole. Moreover, small countries could expect to be bailed out by larger countries. It is unsurprising that the sovereign debt crisis has been worse in small countries such as Greece, Ireland and Portugal.

The tragedy of the Euro is aggravated by the typical short-sightedness of rulers in democracies:[25] politicians tend to focus on the next election rather than the long-term effects of their policies. They use public spending and extend favors to voting factions in order to win the next election. Increasing deficits delays problems into the future and also into the other countries of the Eurozone. EMU leaders know how to externalize the costs of government spending in two dimensions: geographically and temporarily. Geographically, some of the costs are borne in the form of higher prices by the whole Eurozone. Temporarily, the problems resulting from higher deficits are possibly borne by other politicians and only in the remote future. The sovereign debt problems caused by the deficits may require spending cuts imposed by the EMU.

The incentives to run high deficits in the EMU are almost irresistible. As in our printing press example, only if a country runs higher deficits than the others it can benefit. You have to spin the printing press faster than your peers in order to profit from the resulting redistribution. Monetary incomes must rise faster than the purchasing power of the currency falls.

These tragic incentives stem from the unique institutional setup in the EMU: one central bank. These incentives were not unknown when the EMU was planned. The Treaty of Maastricht (Treaty on the European Union), in fact, adopted a no-bailout principle (Article 104b) that states that there will be no bailout in case of fiscal crisis of member states. Along with the no bailout

---

[25] See James Buchanan and Gordon Tullock, *The Calculus of Consent. Logical Foundations of Constitutional Democracy* (Ann Arbor, MI: University of Michigan Press, 1962), and Hoppe, *Democracy: The God that Failed.*

clause came the independence of the ECB. This was to ensure that the central bank would not be used for a bailout.[26]

But political interests and the will to go on with the Euro project have proven stronger than the paper on which the no bailout clause has been written. Moreover, the independence of the ECB does not guarantee that it will not assist a bailout. In fact and as we have seen, the ECB is supporting all governments continuously by accepting their government bonds in its lending operation. It does not matter that it is forbidden for the ECB to buy bonds from governments directly. With the mechanism of accepting bonds as collateral it can finance governments equally well.

There was another attempt to curb the perverse incentives of incurring in excessive deficits. Politicians introduced "managed commons" regulations to reduce the external effects of the tragedy of the commons. The Stability and Growth Pact (SGP) was adopted in 1997 to limit the tragedy in response to German pressure. The pact permits certain "quotas," similar to fishing quotas, for the exploitation of the common central bank. The quota sets limits to the exploitation in that deficits are not allowed to exceed three percent of the GDP and total government debt not sixty percent of the GDP. If these limits had been enforced, the incentive would have been to always be at the maximum of the three percent deficit financed indirectly by the ECB. Countries with a three percent deficit would partially externalize their costs on countries with lower deficits.

However, the regulation of the commons failed. The main problem is that the SGP is an agreement of independent states without credible enforcement. Fishing quotas may be enforced by a particular state. But inflation and deficit quotas of independent states are more difficult to enforce. Automatic sanctions, as initially proposed by the German government, were not included in the SGP. Even though countries violated the

---

[26] See Michael M. Hutchison and Kenneth M. Kletzer, "Fiscal Convergence Criteria, Factor Mobility, and Credibility in Transition to Monetary Union in Europe," in *Monetary and Fiscal Policy in an Integrated Europe*, eds. Barry Eichengreen, Jeffry Frieden and Jürgen von Hagen (Berlin, Heidelberg: Springer, 1995), p. 145.

limits, warnings were issued, but penalties were never enforced. Politically influential countries such as France and Germany, which could have defended the SGP, violated its provisions by having more than three percent deficits from 2003 onward. With a larger number of votes, they and other countries could prevent the imposition of penalties. Consequently, the SGP was a total failure. It could not close the Pandora's Box of a tragedy of the commons. For 2010, all but one member state are expected to violate the three percent maximum limit on deficits. The general European debt ratio to GDP is eighty-eight percent.

THE TRAGEDY OF THE EURO
AND THE CASE OF GREECE

The fiscal developments in Greece are paradigmatic of the tragedy of the Euro and its incentives. When Greece entered the EMU, three factors combined to generate excessive deficits. First, Greece was admitted at a very high exchange rate. At this rate and prevailing wages, many workers were uncompetitive compared with the more highly capitalized workers from Northern countries. To alleviate this problem, the alternatives were to (1) reduce wage rates to increase productivity, (2) increase government spending to subsidize unemployment (by unemployment benefits or early retirement schemes) or (3) employ these uncompetitive directly as public workers. Owing to strong labor unions the first alternative was put aside. Politicians chose the second and third alternatives which implied higher deficits.

Second, by entering the EMU, the Greek government was now supported by an implicit bailout guarantee from the ECB and the other members of the EMU. Interest rates on Greek government bonds fell and approximated German yields. Consequently, the marginal costs of higher deficits were reduced. The interest rates were artificially low. Greece has experienced several defaults in the twentieth century, and has known high inflation rates and deficits as well as a chronic trade deficit. Nevertheless, it was able to indebt itself at almost the same rates as Germany, a country with a conservative fiscal history and an impressive trade surplus.

Third, the tragedy of the commons comes into play. The effects of reckless Greek fiscal behavior could partly be externalized to other members of the EMU as the ECB accepted Greek government bonds as collateral for their lending operations. European banks would buy Greek government bonds (always paying a premium in comparison with German bonds) and use these bonds to receive a loan from the ECB at a lower interest rate (at one percent interest in a highly profitable deal).

Banks bought the Greek bonds because they knew that the ECB would accept these bonds as collateral for new loans. There was a demand for these Greek bonds because the interest rate paid to the ECB was lower than the interest the banks received from the Greek government. Without the acceptance of Greek bonds by the ECB as collateral for its loans, Greece would have had to pay much higher interest rates. In fact, the Greek government has been bailed out or supported by the rest of the EMU in a tragedy of the commons for a long time.

The costs of the Greek deficits were partially shifted to other countries of the EMU. The ECB created new Euros, accepting Greek government bonds as collateral. Greek debts were thus monetized. The Greek government spent the money it received from the bonds sale to win and increase support among its population. When prices started to rise in Greece, money flew to other countries, bidding up prices in the rest of the EMU. In other member states, people saw their buying costs climbing faster than their incomes. This mechanism implied a redistribution in favor of Greece. The Greek government was being bailed out by the rest of the EMU in a constant transfer of purchasing power.

CHAPTER NINE

The EMU as a Conflict-Aggregating System

"If goods don't cross borders, armies will," is an adage often attributed to Frédéric Bastiat and one of the pillar teachings of classical liberalism. When goods are prevented from crossing borders or from being exchanged voluntarily, conflicts arise. In contrast, free trade fosters peace.

In free trade, members of different nations cooperate with each other in harmony. In a voluntary exchange, both parties expect to benefit from it. Imagine that Germans are crazy for Feta cheese and Greeks long for German cars. When Germans buy Feta cheese from Greece and Greeks use their Feta revenues to buy German cars, the exchanges are mutually beneficial ex ante. In the age of division of labor, free trade is a prerequisite of any amicable arrangement between nations.

One possible conflict arises when goods are inhibited or completely forbidden to cross borders. If Germans can only buy Feta cheese at high prices due to tariffs or if the entrance of German cars into Greece is prohibited by law, the seeds for discontent and conflict are sown. If a country fears it will be unable to import essential foods or other commodities due to taxes or blockades, it may prepare for autarchy.

Protectionism and economic nationalism were the main causes of World War II.[1] With the downfall of classical liberalism at the beginning of the twentieth century, free trade was

---

[1] See Ludwig von Mises, *Omnipotent Government: The Rise of the Total State and Total War* (New Haven: Yale University Press, 1944), http://mises.org, ch. 3.

under attack and protectionism was on the rise. Economic nationalism put Germany in a very dangerous position strategically, as she had to import food or commodities such as petroleum. The exposure of her position was shown when a British naval blockade caused the starvation of 100,000 Germans in World War I. After World War I, Adolf Hitler looked for *Lebensraum* and commodities in the east to make Germany self-sufficient in the age of economic nationalism.

Another impediment of free trade and the voluntary exchange of goods is the involuntary transfer of goods from one country to the other. A one-way flow of goods that is involuntary and coercive may sooner or later lead to conflicts between nations. In our example this would be the transfer of German cars to Greece without the corresponding cheese imports from Greece. While German cars flow into Greece, nothing real comes in return; no Feta cheese, no petroleum, no participation in companies, no Greek summer houses, and no vacations at Greek beaches.

A historical example of an involuntary one-way flow of goods is provided by the German reparations after World War I, when gold and goods were transferred to Allied countries under the threat of a gun. Germans at the time were outraged by this one-way transfer of goods. Hitler was elected on the promise of getting rid of the hated Treaty of Versailles and war reparations in particular. These reparations, seen as an additional violation of the voluntary exchange of goods, were factors leading to World War II.[2]

The founders of the European integration after World War II, Konrad Adenauer, Robert Schuman, Paul Henri Spaak, and Alcide de Gaspari, knew the importance of free trade for lasting peace.[3] The horrors of war were very close to them. They wanted to create an environment in Europe that would put an end to the recurring wars and foster peace.

---

[2] On the hunger blockade see Ralph Raico, "The Blockade and Attempted Starvation of Germany," Mises.org daily article (May 7, 2010) [C. Paul Vincent, *The Politics of Hunger: Allied Blockade of Germany, 1915–1919*, (Athens, OH: Ohio University Press, 1985). This review was first published in the *Review of Austrian Economics* 3 no. 1.]

[3] See Ginsberg, *Demystifying the European Union*, p. 387.

Their efforts have been a success; there has not been a war in Europe between member states of the European Union. In order to create this peaceful environment, the founders established a free trade zone fostering voluntary exchange. Mutually beneficial cooperation creates bonds, understanding, trust, dependency, and friendship. Yet, the construction was not perfect. While the Treaty of Rome established free movement of capital, labor and goods, unfortunately, the field was left open for the involuntary transfers of goods.

There are two main mechanisms by which wealth, i.e., goods, are redistributed between member states in one direction, thereby creating cracks into the harmonious cooperation of Europeans.

The first mechanism for one-way transfers of goods is the official redistribution system. The Rome Treaty already contained the goal of "regional development," i.e., redistribution. Yet there was little action in this area until the 1970s. Today it is the second largest spending area of the EU. One third of its budget is dedicated to "harmonizing" wealth. The European Regional Development Fund (ERDF) was established in 1975. It spends money in the "structural funds" to finance regional development projects.

The other pillar of the direct EU redistribution policy is the idea of "cohesion funds," instituted in 1993 to harmonize structures of countries and make their entrance into the EMU feasible. Cohesion funds are only open to countries with a GDP that is below ninety percent of the EU average. They are used to finance environmental projects or transportation networks. Their main beneficiaries have been Ireland and Southern European countries.[4]

The Dutch are the biggest net payers to the European Union, followed by the Danes and Germans.[5] From 1995 to 2003, Germany paid net €76 billion into the coffers of the European Union.[6] In 2009, the German government transferred €15

---

[4] Ibid., pp. 257–260.

[5] See Dutchnews.nl, "Dutch are Biggest EU Net Payers: PVV," (January 14, 2010), http://www.dutchnews.nl.

[6] Hannich, *Die kommende Euro-Katastrophe*, p. 30.

billion to the European Union.[7] The redistribution of wealth among member states is a potential source of conflict: goods are effectively transferred without anything in return. Cars roll toward Greece with no cheese in return.

The second mechanism for the involuntary one-way flow of goods is the market for money. As discussed, there exists a monopolistic producer of base money, which is the European Central Bank. The ECB redistributes wealth by creating new money and distributing it unequally to the national governments on the basis of their deficits.

The national government spends more than it receives in taxes. To pay for the difference, i.e., the deficit, the national government prints government bonds. The bonds are sold to the banking system, which in turn takes the bonds to the ECB and pledge them as collateral for loans made through the creation of new money. In this way, national governments can practically print money. Their bonds are as good as money as long the ECB accepts them as collateral. As a consequence, the supply of Euros increases. The first receivers of the new money, the national governments running deficits, can still enjoy the old, lower prices. As the new money spreads to other countries, prices are bid up in the whole European Monetary Union (EMU). Later receivers of new money see their buying prices increase before incomes starts to increase.

To use a real world example: the Greek economy is not competitive at the exchange rate with which it entered the Eurozone. Wages would have to fall to make it competitive. But wages are rigid due to privileged labor unions. Greece has maintained this situation by running public deficits and printing government bonds to pay unproductive people high wage rates: its public servants and the unemployed. Those who receive government benefits may use this new money to buy ever more expensive German cars. The rest of Europe becomes poorer as car prices increase. There is one way transfer of cars from Germany to Greece. The means used to pay for the cars are produced in a coercive and involuntary way: the money monopoly.

---

[7] Bandulet, *Die letzten Jahre des Euro,* p. 107.

When commenting on the Maastricht Treaty and the introduction of the Euro, the parallels to a reparation induced transfer of goods were noted in the French newspaper, *Le Figaro*, on September 18, 1992: "'Germany will pay' people said in the 1920s. Today she is paying: Maastricht is the Treaty of Versailles without war."[8]

It was not only the Treaty of Versailles that created clashes. The monetary arrangement established by the Maastricht Treaty breeds conflicts as well, as we have already seen. The single currency institutionalizes conflict as the struggle for control of the money supply intensifies. As Greece's structural problems remain unresolved and its government debt reaches extraordinary levels, Greece struggles to place new debts on the markets—even though the ECB still accepts Greek government bonds as collateral (even if they are rated as junk). The market has begun to doubt the willingness and capacity of the rest of the EMU to stabilize the Greek government.

The result is the bailout and transfer of funds from the EMU to Greece in the form of subsidized loans. The process of the bailout implying involuntary one-way transfers of goods has provoked contempt and hatred on government and civilian levels, especially between Germany and Greece.

German newspapers called Greeks "liars" when their government falsified statistics.[9] One German tabloid asked why Germans retire at age sixty-seven, yet the government transfers funds to Greece so Greeks can retire at an earlier age.[10] In turn, Greek newspapers continue to accuse Germany of atrocities during World War II and claim that reparations are still owed them.

---

[8] Quoted in Roland Baader, *Die Euro-Katastrophe*, p. 163.

[9] See Alkman Granitsas and Paris Costas, "Greek and German Media Tangle over Crisis," *The Wall Street Journal* (February 24, 2010), http://online.wsj.com.

[10] See Hoeren and Santen, "Griechenland-Pleite."

CHAPTER TEN

The Ride Toward Collapse

When the financial crisis hit, governments responded with the typical Keynesian recipe: deficit spending. With an accelerating course of events, the EMU drove into the abyss of its breakup. We begin our story a few months after the collapse of Lehman Brothers, when the effects of the crisis on government deficits started affecting sovereign ratings.

At the beginning, Greece was the main focus of attention. In January of 2009, the rating agency S&P cut Greece's rating to an A−, the same day the government gave in to striking farmers, promising them additional subsidies of €0.5 billion. Problems spread. By the end of April 2009, the EU Commission started investigating excessive deficits in Spain, Ireland, Greece and France. By October, the rating agency, Fitch, reduced Greece's rating to an A− as well.

At the end of 2009 several European countries acknowledged that they had excessive deficits.

Responses to budgetary problems varied. Ireland announced spending cuts of ten percent of the GDP. The Spanish government did not cut spending at all, nor did Greece.

At the end of 2009, the new government in Greece announced that its deficits would be at a record 12.7 percent—more than three times higher than the 3.7 percent announced earlier in 2009. On December 1, finance ministers of the EMU agreed on harsher action with regard to the Greek government, and on

December 8, Fitch lowered its ranking to BBB+. S&P followed suit and downgraded Greece.

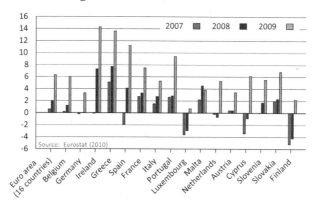

Graph 9: Deficits as a percentage of GDP in Euro area 2007, 2008, and 2009

As a first response, newly elected Prime Minister, Georgios Papandreou, did not increase pensions as promised, but rather increased taxes to reduce the deficit. The interest rates that Greece had to pay on its debts had started to increase in the fall of 2009 and began troubling the markets. German Minister of Finance, Wolfgang Schäuble, stated that Greece had lived beyond its means for years, and that Germans could not pay the price.

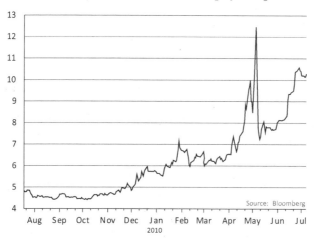

Graph 10: Yield of Greek ten-year bond (August 2009–July 2010)

The market started to have doubts about Greece's being able to repay its debts. And it was feared that the ECB would stop financing the Greek deficit indirectly. If the ECB would stop accepting Greek bonds as collateral for loans, no one would buy Greek bonds. The government would have to default on its obligations.

The ECB had lowered the required minimum rating for its open market operations from A– to BBB– in response to the financial crisis. The reduction was supposed to be an exception and was to expire at the end of 2010. Due to budgetary problems, Greece was in danger of losing the minimum A– rating. What would happen in 2011 when Greece's rating would not meet the A– minimum?

On January 12, 2010, the ECB cast doubt on the deficit data provided by the Greek government. Irregularities had made the accuracy of Greek statistics questionable. On January 14, S&P actually cut the long-term rating of Greece to A– and put Spain, Portugal, and Ireland on a negative outlook due to their budgetary problems. On the same day, Greece announced a reduction of its deficit of €10.6 billion. The reduction came from tax increases (€7 billion) and spending cuts (€3.6 billion). The deficit was to be reduced from 12.7 percent to 8.7 percent of the GDP. Papandreou also announced a freeze on salaries for state employees, thereby breaking a promise he had made before his election. The state workers' union announced strikes on February 10.

On January 15, Jean-Claude Trichet, ECB president, still maintained a hard money rhetoric: "We will not change our collateral framework for the sake of any particular country. Our collateral framework applies to all countries concerned."[1] Market participants interpreted this statement as a pledge that the ECB would not extend the exceptional reduction of the required minimum rating to BBB– just to save the Greek government. Along the same line, chief economist of the ECB, Jürgen Stark, stated in January that markets were wrong in believing that other member states would bail Greece out.

---

[1] See Tobias Bayer, "Hilfen für Hellas: Kehrtwende kratzt an Glaubwürdigkeit der EZB," *Financial Times Deutschland* (2010), http://www.ftd.de.

By the end of January, financial markets started selling Greek bonds at a faster pace—after the Deutsche Bank warned that Greece's default would be more disastrous than the defaults of Argentina in 2001 or Russia in 1998. As the pressure intensified, Papandreou announced additional measures that would, according to an estimate by economists of the bank, HSBC, cut the deficit a further 0.4 percent.[2] In addition, Papandreou declared his intention of bringing the Greek deficit back to three percent by 2012. The EU Commission backed his plan. The EU back up was significant: it helped Papandreou internally. Politically, he could shift the blame to the EU and speculators. He could present himself as if he were obliged by the EU to make the unpopular budget cuts. Moreover, he stated that evil speculators had brought this situation upon Greece: "Greece is in the centre of a speculative game aimed at the Euro. It is our national duty to stop the attempts to push our country to the edge of the cliff."[3] Greece, of course, would make sacrifices to save the Euro.

In February of 2010, it became public that the investment bank Goldman Sachs had helped the Greek government mask the true extent of its deficit by using derivatives. The Greek government had never fulfiled the Maastricht rule of sixty percent debt of the GDP, nor had it, starting in 1991, fulfiled the 3% deficit limit. Only balance sheet cosmetics, like leaving out military spending or hospital debts made Greece formally fulfil the limit for a single year. The Goldman Sachs derivatives disguised a loan as a swap. Greece issued bonds in foreign currencies. Goldman sold Greece currency swaps at a fictional exchange rate. Thus Greece received more Euros than the market value of the foreign currencies it had received from the bond sale. Once the bond matured, the Greek government had to pay back the bond with Euros. Goldman Sachs received a

---

[2] See Maria Petrakis and Meera Louis, "EU Backs Greek Deficit Plan: Papandreou Offers Cuts," *Bloomberg* (February 3, 2010), http://noir.bloomberg.com.

[3] Ibid.

generous commission for the deal that concealed the interest rate.[4]

On February 16, the Economic and Financial Affairs Council (Ecofin), composed of economics and finance ministers of the EU, imposed an adjustment plan on the Greek government in exchange for unspecified support. As the days went by the Greek government became nervous, demanding concrete support by other member states. If no support were offered, Greece would ask the IMF for cheap loans. The engagement of the IMF would have been very embarrassing for the greater Euro project. Would the EMU need the IMF to solve its problems? Confidence in the Euro was further reduced.

On February 24, S&P declared that it might downgrade Greece one or two notches within the month. At this time only Moody's maintained a rating sufficient to make Greek bonds eligible as collateral under normal conditions.

At the end of February, President Papandreou met with Josef Ackermann, CEO of the Deutsche Bank. Ackermann was interested in solving the Greek problem. The Deutsche Bank owned Greek government debt and a default could bring down the whole European banking system, including the Deutsche Bank. After the meeting, Ackermann proposed to Jens Weidmann, adviser to Angela Merkel, that private banks, Germany and France each lend €7.5 billion to Greece. The proposal was denied. The German government feared a complaint of unconstitutionality. A bailout would violate article 125 of the Treaty on the functioning of the European Union, which states that member states are not responsible for other states' debts. Most importantly, the German population was against a bailout. Merkel wanted to wait with a solution to the problem until after an important election in the Federal State of North-Rhine Westphalia, which was scheduled for May.

On February 28, Merkel still publicly denied the possibility of a German bailout for Greece: "We have a treaty which rules

---

[4] See Beat Balzli, "How Goldman Sachs Helped Greece to Mask its True Debt," *Spiegel online* (2010), http://www.spiegel.de.

out the possibility of bailing out other nations."[5] Her ministers, Brüderle and Westerwelle, confirmed this point of view. At the same time, the EU demanded that the Greek government reduce its deficit an extra 4.8 billion Euros. The yield of Greek bonds rose to seven percent.

On March 3, Papandreou agreed to the demanded extra €4.8 billion, or two percent, deficit cuts. He announced higher fuel, tobacco, and sales taxes, as well as a thirty percent cut of the three bonus-salary payments to civil servants. Greek public workers had been better off than their peers in other countries. In Greece, twelve percent of the GDP was paid to public workers in 2009, a figure which was up by two percent from 2000, and two percent higher than the EU's average. Nevertheless, Greek unions announced new strikes.

In return for the "cuts," Papandreou demanded "European solidarity," i.e., money from other states. The Greek "cuts" gave Merkel some of the political capital she needed to sell the bailout to Germans. The situation became more pressing every day: in May, twenty billion of Greek debt would mature, and it was not clear if markets would refinance these debts at acceptable rates.

On March 5 and 7, Papandreou met with Sarkozy and Merkel to rally their support. At the same time, fears were rising that revenues from the Greek tax increases might remain short of projections. S&P dropped its negative outlook of the Greek rating as it became clearer that the EU would finally intervene in favor of the Greek government. To forestall market panics in the future, Axel Weber, a member of the governing council of the ECB, called for an institutionalization of emergency aid.

On March 15, finance ministers from the Euro states met to discuss a possible bailout of the Greek government. Nothing new resulted. Ministers only reiterated that Greek cuts were sufficient to fulfil the 2010 projected aim. Three days later, Merkel confirmed that any bailout plan would have to incorporate a provision for expulsion of states that did not comply with the rules. And she repeated that investors should

---

[5] See Andreas Illmer, "Merkel Rules Out German Bailout for Greece," *Deutsche Welle* (March 1, 2010), http://www.dw-world.de.

not expect a Greek aid pact. At the same time, Zapatero and Sarkozy demanded an economic government for the EU.

On March 25, the ECB and EMU nations acted together for the first time: Trichet, in contrast to his January statement, announced that emergency collateral rules would be extended through 2011. Greek bonds regained the potential to serve as collateral. On the same day, EU nations agreed, in cooperation with the IMF, on a bailout for Greece. Germany had demanded IMF involvement. No details of the bailout were made concrete and markets were left in the dark. While the German population was against a bailout, its political class made similar arguments to those it used when arguing in favor of the introduction of the Euro. According to Daniel Hannan, a British member of the European parliament, one German politician had stated that World War II might start again were Greece not bailed out.[6]

On April 11, two days after Fitch had downgraded Greece to BBB–, the interest rate of Greek bonds rose to eight percent. Finally, the German government agreed to subsidize €30 billion EMU loans to Greece, with an additional €15 billion coming from the IMF. Markets plunged. Resistance to budget cuts in Greece increased.

Civil servants went on strike on April 22. On the same day, the EU announced that the Greek deficit in 2009 was even higher than previously reported. Instead of 12.7 percent, it was 13.6 percent with total debts at 115 percent of the GDP. In response, Moody's cut Greece's rating one notch, to A3. Papandreou maintained that the data revision would not affect his plan to reduce the deficit in 2010 to 8.7 percent. Greek, Spanish and Portuguese bonds fell.

The next day, the Greek government was forced to activate the bailout package of €45 billion, the details of which had been worked out in the two days prior. The Greek government got access to €30 billion from Euro-nations in a three year facility at 5 percent, and €15 billion from the IMF at lower rates. Greece had

---

[6] See Daniel Hannan, "Germans! Stop Being Ripped Off!" *Telegraph.co.uk* (March 27, 2010), http://blogs.telegraph.co.uk.

to have access to the facility; on May 19, €8.5 billion came due, and markets would probably not refinance.

On April 27, the National Bank of Greece SA, the country's largest lender, and EFG Eurobank Ergasias were downgraded to junk status by S&P. On the same day, Greece's country rating was downgraded to junk status. S&P also downgraded Portugal from A+ to A−. One day later, S&P downgraded Spain from AA+ to AA.

Things accelerated at the beginning of May. It was obvious that the €45 billion bailout of Greece would not be sufficient to avert its default. On May 2, Euro-region ministers agreed to an even greater bailout of loans totaling €110 billion at a rate of around five percent. The second rescue package was supposed to bring the country through the next three years. In line with the capital in the ECB, 27.92 percent of the loans would come from Germany.

Country	Percentage of bailout
Germany	27.92
France	20.97
Italy	18.42
Spain	12.24
Netherlands	5.88
Belgium	3.58
Austria	2.86
Portugal	2.58
Finland	1.85
Ireland	1.64
Slovakia	1.02
Slovenia	0.48
Luxembourg	0.26
Cyprus	0.20
Malta	0.09

Table 1: Percentage of bailout per country
Source: ECB 2010

Merkel agreed to the bailout despite the impending election. In return, the Greek government agreed to cut public wages and pensions again and to raise the sales tax to twenty-three percent. Fears began to spread that Spain would need a bailout as well.

A second collaboration between the EMU ministers and the ECB occurred on the same day. The independence of the ECB began evaporating when it announced it would drop all rating requirements for Greek government bonds. The ECB would accept Greek bonds as collateral no matter what. By contradicting its previous approach and becoming an executor of politics, the ECB lost a lot of credibility. The ECB presented itself more and more as the inflationary machine—in service of high politics—that had been intended by French and other Latin politicians. The European stock index, Eurostoxx 50, surged ten percent immediately.

On May 4, the Greek government created a fund to support its tumbling banking system. The word was that Spain was facing an imminent downgrade, but the rumor was denied by Spanish President, José Luis Rodriguez Zapatero. European stock markets plunged. Athens fell 6.7 percent, Madrid 5.4 percent. The following day, Moody's cut Portugal's rating two notches to A–. Demonstrators set fire to a bank in Athens, causing the death of three. Financial markets were shocked.

By May 6, Trichet still resisted pressure to buy government bonds of troubled European governments outright. Axel Weber also spoke out against that option. The Dow Jones crashed 1,000 points in a few minutes and recovered half of its losses by the end of the day. The Euro followed suit.

The next day the Eurosystem was on the verge of collapse. Yields on Spanish, Greek, and Portuguese bonds increased sharply. Observers maintain that trading in European bonds came to a hold almost completely in the afternoon. Not even French bonds were liquid.[7] In the monthly report of the ECB for June 2010, the central bank admitted the threat of a total collapse on May 6 and 7. The ECB stated that the danger had been greater than after the collapse of Lehman Brothers in September 2008. It admitted a dramatic rise in the bankruptcy probability of two

---

[7] Telebörse.de, "EZB öffnet Büchse der Pandora," *Dossier* (May 10, 2010), http://www.teleboerse.de.

or more major European banking groups.[8] Apparently banks that had invested in Mediterranean sovereign debts had severe problems with refinancing. Money markets dried up.

According to the newspaper *Welt am Sonntag*, German bankers received panic calls from French colleagues asking them to pressure the ECB to buy Greek government bonds.[9] Even President Obama called Chancellor Merkel when money flows from the U.S. to Europe dried up. May 7 was a Friday. Politicians and central bankers were able to regroup over the weekend and prevent a total collapse.

On the same day (but ignored by markets), the German parliament passed a law permitting loans in favor of the Greek government. On the weekend, the German Federal Constitutional Court dismissed a claim brought forward by four German professors, the same four who had taken action against the introduction of the Euro (Karl Albrecht Schachtschneider, Wilhelm Hankel, Wilhelm Nölling, and Joachim Starbatty). They argued that the bailout would breach article 125 of the Treaty on the Functioning of the EU, which states that no country is responsible for the debt of other member states.

On Sunday, the coalition forming the German government lost dramatically in the election in the federal state North-Rhine Westphalia. Merkel had wanted to delay the bailout of Greece until after the election. But after the acceleration of events she sacrificed the victory in order to save the Euro. She cancelled her appearances on the campaign to fly to Brussels, where the European Council finance ministers were meeting.

Sarkozy and Berlusconi also found it necessary to attend the meeting of the finance ministers. They maintained that a new rescue fund to bail out more countries would be necessary. Merkel regarded this as a step into a transfer union. The EU Commission would gain power and the Southern states would benefit from subsidized loans from richer nations. She resisted in

---

[8] See Helga Einecke and Martin Hesse, "Kurz vor der Apokalypse," *Süddeutsche Zeitung* (June 16, 2010), http://www.sueddeutsche.de and ECB, *Monthly Bulletin: June* (2010), http://www.ecb.int, pp. 37–40.

[9] Jörg Eigendorf et al., "Chronologie des Scheiterns," *Welt.online* (May 16, 2010), http://www.welt.de.

the beginning. In a dinner on Friday evening, Trichet explained the gloomy severity of the situation.

Merkel succeeded in delaying the final decision until the Sunday after the election. Tellingly, on May 8 she was in Moscow to celebrate 65 years of German defeat against the Soviet Union. Negotiations began again on Sunday afternoon. Trichet attended again, even though he was the President of a supposedly independent ECB. German officials called him an attachment of the French ministry of Finance. The German minister of Finance, Wolfgang Schäuble, did not attend, as he had been taken to a hospital. (The official explanation was an allergic reaction to a drug.) Negotiations were difficult. Even Obama and Bernanke intervened and called Merkel demanding a massive rescue package.

Politicians from Finland, Austria, and the Netherlands took Germany's side in the negotiations. Interests were clear. Governments with high deficits and spending were rebelling against states with lower deficits and hard money governments that were their potential creditors.

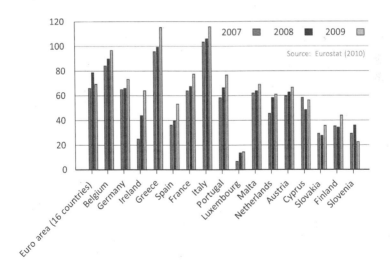

. **Graph 11:** Debts as a percentage of GDP in Euro area 2007, 2008 and 2009

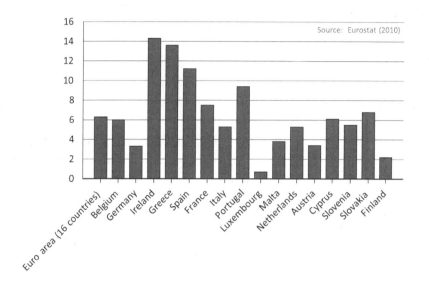

Graph 12: Deficits as a percentage of GDP in Euro area 2009

While Greece was relatively unimportant due to its small size, larger debtors had gotten into severe trouble in May. Banks head-quartered in the Eurozone had €144 billion exposure to Greece, but €507 billion to Spain. The new rescue package was instituted in order to prevent a default of Portuguese and Spanish debtors that would have affected German and especially French banks adversely. The French government, however, had more interest in the bailout than the German government.

The direct exposure of French banks to government debts of Portugal, Ireland, Greece and Spain was higher than the exposure of German banks as can be seen in Table 2.

	French banks	German banks
Spain	€33 billion	€23 billion
Greece	€22 billion	€16 billion
Portugal	€15 billion	€7 billion
Ireland	€4 billion	€0.7 billion

Table 2: Exposure to government debt of French and German banks (as of December 31, 2009)

The total debt that French banks held for Portugal, Ireland, Greece, and Spain at the end of 2009, public and private, was €344 billion. German banks held almost as much: €324 billion. Spain's share was the majority, with €173 billion in the case of French banks, and €141 billion in the case of German banks. Defaults of Spanish banks or the Spanish government would have had adverse effects on German and French banks. A default of Portuguese banks or its government could, in turn, take down Spanish banks that held €77 billion in Portuguese debt.[10]

The final agreement, the so-called "emergency parachute," provided loans of up to €750 billion for troubled governments. The EU Commission provided €60 billion for the package. Once these funds were exhausted, countries could get loans guaranteed by the member states of up to €440 billion. Member states would guarantee loans based on their capital in the ECB. Germany would guarantee up to €123 billion. The IMF also provided loans of up to €250 billion.

In exchange for these guarantees, the socialist governments of Spain and Portugal accepted deficit cuts. The Spanish government announced a cut in civil servant salaries and delayed an increase in pensions. The Portuguese government announced a cut in wages for top government officials and a plan to increase taxes. Presumably pressured by the German government, Italy and even France would announce deficit cuts later in May. The European Commission assessed these cuts and declared them to be steps into the right direction.

As the Spanish newspaper, *El País*, claimed, Sarkozy had threatened to break the German-French alliance if Merkel would not cooperate with a "parachute" that favored French banks with the biggest part of Mediterranean debt, or to abandon the Euro all together. The French exit from the Eurozone if Germany would not pay, may well be called as one of the greatest bluffs in history.

---

[10] See Bank for International Settlements, "International Banking and Financial Markets Development," *BIS Quarterly Report* (June, 2010), pp. 18–22.

Merkel herself stated that: "If the Euro fails, the idea of European integration fails."[11] Her argument is a non sequitur. Naturally, one can have open borders, free trade and an integrated Europe without a common central bank. Here Merkel showed herself to be a defender of the socialist version of Europe.

With the new "parachute," the Eurozone had made it apparent that it was a transfer union. Before the "parachute," redistribution had been concealed by the complex monetary mechanisms of the Eurosystem. Now outright fiscal support from one country to the other was made more obvious. German taxpayers were suddenly guaranteeing for around €148 billion or more than 60 percent of government revenues. As so often after World War I Germans had to tribute but did not have a say.[12]

Over the course of these important days, European central bankers cooperated with politicians. Before markets reopened on Monday, May 10, the ECB announced that it would purchase government bonds on the market, thereby crossing a line many thought it would never cross. The decision to buy government bonds was not unanimous. Bundesbankers Axel Weber and Jürgen Stark resisted the decision and were supported by Nout Wellink, President of De Nederlandsche Bank, the traditional ally of the Bundesbank. Trichet, despite his denial the previous week, maintained that the ECB had not been pressured and remained independent. The ECB claimed its measure would not be inflationary; the bank would sterilize the increase in the monetary base by accepting term deposits by banks. The ECB would thereby behave as a typical bank does, by borrowing

---

[11] See Spiegel.online, "Deutschland weist Bericht über Sarkozy-Ausraster zurück," *Spiegel.online* (May 14, 2010), http://www.spiegel.de.

[12] The list of German tributes is long. Only in September 2010 the German government paid the last debts resulting from reparations for World War I. Already before the "parachute," Germany paid 89 percent more to the EU than it would have to pay considering per capita income. The excess pay amounted to €70 billion in the decade following 1999. See Henkel, *Rettet unser Geld!*, p. 139.

short and lending long. For private banks this behavior is quite risky as the short term debt must be rolled over.[13] For the ECB this risk consists in a failure to attract sufficient deposits which would result in inflationary monetary expansion. Of course, the ECB could attempt to attract deposits by raising rates but then the higher interest rates would pose problems for indebted governments and companies alike. The magazine *Spiegel* commented later in May on further irritation on the part of Bundesbankers.[14] Because of the €750 billion parachute, some Bundesbankers did not see any reason for the purchase of government bonds on the part of the ECB (€40 billion up to this point). They suspected a conspiracy. German banks had promised German finance minister Wolfgang Schäuble that they would hold on to Greek bonds until 2013. French banks and insurances companies, having €70–€80 billion in Greek bonds on their books, were exploiting the occasion to sell Greek, Spanish and Portuguese government bonds as Trichet sustained bond prices via central bank purchases.

The result of the coordinated action of the government of the EMU and the ECB was a de facto coup d'état. The principles of the economic and monetary union as originally established were abolished. A new institution with the name European Financial Stability Facility (EFSF), headquartered in Luxembourg, was granted the possibility of selling debt to bail out member states. The new institution could operate independently. Member states would only be involved in that they would guarantee the debt issued by the EFSF. With its own bureaucracy, the EFSF will probably increase its power in a push for further centralization. The EFSF provokes and provides incentives toward over-indebtedness and the bailouts it was instituted to alleviate.

---

[13] On maturity mismatching, how it is promoted by interventions such as the privilege of fractional reserve banking, central banking and government bailout guarantees, and the resulting distortions in the real economy see Philipp Bagus, "Austrian Business Cycle Theory: Are 100 Percent Reserves Sufficient to Prevent a Business Cycle?" *Libertarian Papers*, 2 (2, 2010).

[14] See Wolfgang Reuter, "German Central Bankers Suspect French Intrigue," *Spiegel.online* (May 31, 2010), http://www.spiegel.de.

Moreover, if the EFSF wants to issue more than the agreed upon amount of debt, it needs only the approval of the finance ministers of the Eurozone. The increase in power does not have to pass in parliament. The enabling act of May 9 changed the institutional structure of the EMU forever. A union of stability as imagined by Northern states was substituted by an open transfer union.

As a consequence of both the fiscal and monetary interventions in favor of troubled debtor governments, stock markets around the world rallied. The Eurostoxx 50 climbed 10.4 percent. Spanish, Greek, Portuguese, and Italian bonds climbed while German bonds fell; the German government had effectively guaranteed the debts of Latin countries.

In the weeks that followed, European leaders tried to revamp the Stability and Growth Pact. The SGP provided for fines of as much as 0.5 percent of the GDP if countries did not get their budgets back into compliance with the three percent ceiling. Yet despite several infringements, no country had been fined during the Euro's eleven year lifespan. After failing to stay within the limit for three years in a row, the governments of Germany and France had teamed up in 2005 to dilute the rules.

Now new penalties were being discussed: sanctions and cutting off EU development-aid funds for exceeding the three percent deficit mark. In June, Merkel proposed also a removal of voting rights as a penalty for infringements, but she was not able to push her proposal through. Another initiative that failed was a proposal made by the EU Commission for more coordination of budgetary plans before they were voted on by national parliaments. Germany, France and Spain objected to this plan as it would reduce their sovereignty.

After the apparent tranquilization of markets, Spain lost its AAA credit grade at Fitch Ratings on May 28. In June, Greece accelerated the privatization process by selling stakes in public companies. Insurance for sovereign debts increased even for Germany, which announced its own measures to reduce its deficits of €80 billion by 2014.

Meanwhile the problems of the banking system grew. The price of government bonds had been falling. Banks were in a dilemma. Selling government bonds would have revealed losses and reduced confidence in governments. The banking system and the government sector were more connected than ever. Defaults in any one of them could cause defaults in the other. If Greece defaulted on its obligations, banks holding Greek government bonds might become insolvent. These insolvent banks could trigger the collapse of other banks or prompt a bailout of their respective governments, pushing their respective governments toward default as well. If, however, banks suffered losses and went bankrupt, they would probably prompt the intervention of their governments to save the national banking system. This bailout would imply more government debt, an acceleration of the sovereign debt crisis, and possibly debt's being pushed beyond a sustainable level. A panic in sovereign debt markets and government default could be the consequence.

In June, Spain moved into the market's spotlight. A partial Greek default or debt restructuring was already assumed and discounted by markets. A Spanish default, however, would be a bigger problem. Bad news turned up. Spanish banks, especially the smaller Cajas, could not refinance themselves any more at the interbank market, but were kept afloat by loans from the ECB alone. Their dependence on ECB lending had increased to a record €86 billion in May. Rumors spread that the Spanish government was about to tap the bailout facility. This was promptly denied by Spanish authorities.

On June 14, Moody's downgraded Greek government bonds to junk status. Greek banks were losing not only credit lines from other banks but also their own deposit base, which had shrunk seven percent in one year as Greeks shifted their funds outside its banking system. Greek banks were taking €85 billion in loans from the ECB, pledging mostly Greek government bonds as collateral.[15] At the same time, the ECB kept buying government bonds which already totaled €47 billion.

---

[15] See Ambrose Evans-Pritchard, "Axa Fears 'Fatal-Flaw' Will Destroy Eurozone," *Telegraph.co.uk* (June 14, 2010), http://www.telegraph.co.uk.

Things calmed down somewhat in July; there was also some bad news. The Greek government cancelled the scheduled issuance of twelve month government bonds, relying on short maturities (twenty-six weeks) and rescue funds. Strikes in the country did not end, harming the tourism industry. On July 13, Moody's lowered Portugal's credit rating by two notches: to A1. But good news prevailed. The announcement of a stress test of European banks calmed markets in the expectation of transparency and the solution of the bank problems. The ECB kept buying government bonds and expressed concern over insufficient savings measures of deficit countries. Spain managed to refinance important amounts on the market. The Greek government voted for moving the retirement age to sixty-five years. Slovakia, the last country resisting the €750 billion parachute, finally approved the plan.

A diagram of the Euro exchange rate maps out our story.

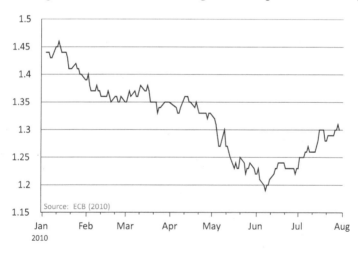

Graph 13: Euro/dollar (January–August 2010)

At the same time, the depreciation of the Euro is an illustration of the importance of the quality of a currency.[16] The quantity

---

[16] Philipp Bagus, "The Fed's Dilemma," *Mises.org daily* (October 8, 2009), http://mises.org.

of the Euro did not change dramatically in relation to the dollar in these months. But its quality deteriorated substantially.

The quality of a currency is its capacity to fulfil the basic functions of money, i.e., to serve as a good medium of exchange, a store of value, and a unit of account. Important factors of the quality of a currency are the institutional setup of the central bank, and its staff and its assets, among others. The assets of a central bank are important because they back up its liabilities, i.e., the currency, and can be used to defend the currency internally, externally, or in a monetary reform.[17]

During the first half of 2010, the capacity of the Euro to serve as a store of value became more and more dubious. In fact, it was not clear if the Euro would survive the sovereign debt crisis at all. Confidence in the Euro's capacity to serve as a store of value was shaken. The credibility of the ECB in particular was reduced substantially. Trichet had denied that special collateral rules would be applied to certain countries, or that the ECB would buy outright government bonds. In both cases he had broken his word. This changed the perception of the ECB dramatically.

At the Euro's birth, the question was if the Euro would be a Germanic-Euro or a Latin-Euro. Would the ECB operate in the tradition of the Bundesbank or of the central banks of Mediterranean Europe? The events of spring 2010 pointed ever more to the second option. The ECB was not primarily focused on the stability of the value of the Euro and resistant to political interests, but rather a loyal servant to politics in a transfer union. The monetary union had become a transfer union where monetary policy backed a transfer of wealth within Europe.

Not only did Trichet's breaking his word diminish the quality of the Euro, but he crossed the Rubicon in the eyes of many by buying government bonds outright (even though, economically, there is not a substantial difference in accepting government bonds as collateral for lending operations).

---

[17] Philipp Bagus and Markus Schiml, "A Cardiograph of the Dollar's Quality: Qualitative Easing and the Federal Reserve Balance Sheet During the Subprime Crisis," *Prague Economic Papers* 19 (3, 2010): pp. 195–217.

Another factor weighing on the quality of the Euro was that the voices of former Bundesbankers lost influence in the council of the ECB. Latin bankers dominated. Axel Weber of Germany protested the decision of the ECB to buy government bonds, but to no avail.

Besides the change of the perception of the ECB toward a more inflationary central bank, another factor affected the quality of the Euro negatively: qualitative easing.[18] Qualitative easing describes a monetary policy used by central banks that leads to a reduction of the average quality of the assets backing the monetary base (or the CB's liabilities). By buying government bonds of troubled countries, the average quality of assets backing the Euro was diminished.

It makes a difference if for €1000 issued by the ECB, it holds on its asset side €1000 worth of gold, €1000 worth of German government bonds, or €1000 Euro worth of Greek government bonds. These assets are of different quality and liquidity, affecting the quality of the Euro.

In the end, the ECB's balance sheet accumulated more and more problematic government bonds that the ECB had bought from the banking system. The ECB used qualitative easing to prop up the banking system by absorbing its bad assets and the quality of the Euro was reduced. A default of Greece or other countries would consequently imply important losses for the ECB. These would further diminish confidence in the Euro and could make recapitalization necessary.[19]

---

[18] See Philipp Bagus and Markus Schiml, "New Modes of Monetary Policy: Qualitative Easing by the Fed," *Economic Affairs* 29 (2, 2009): pp. 46–49, for more information. For case studies of the balance sheet policies of the FED see Bagus and Schiml, "A Cardiograph of the Dollar's Quality," and "New Modes of Monetary Policy"; and for the policies of the ECB, Philipp Bagus and David Howden, "The Federal Reserve and Eurosystem's Balance Sheet Policies During the Subprime Crisis: A Comparative Analysis," *Romanian Economic and Business Review* 4 (3, 2009): pp. 165–185, and Philipp Bagus and David Howden, "Qualitative Easing in Support of a Tumbling Financial System: A Look at the Eurosystem's Recent Balance Sheet Policies," *Economic Affairs* 21 (4, 2009): pp. 283–300.

[19] For the recapitalization possibility and possible problems see Bagus and Howden, "The Federal Reserve and Eurosystem's Balance Sheet Policies," and "Qualitative Easing in Support of a Tumbling Financial System."

At the same time, the economic condition of governments and the quality of their bonds used as collateral for lending operations deteriorated. If a bank were to default on its loans, the ECB would be left with collateral that was falling in value and quality. The Euro only stabilized in July when the Spanish government saw that it would be able to refinance itself on the markets, German industry published excellent results, and the US recovery was slower than had been expected.

Further help was provided by a stress test of the European banking system. Via simulation, the test analysed how European banks would resist a partial sovereign default. Unrealistic assumptions were chosen to provide the desired outcome: the majority of banks passed the test—an important marketing coup. The stress tests only addressed the banks' trading book positions. The assumption was made that the bonds would not default, and hence there was no need to consider any impact on the hold-to-maturity books of the banks. In addition, the tests assumed very low losses, such as a mere 23% discount for Greek bonds. Moreover, it did not take into account the interconnectivity of events. If Greece would default this could trigger a default of Portugal and then Spain and so on. The assumption that the discount could be contained to 23% on Greek bonds was highly unrealistic. Furthermore, the stress test did not take into account eventually losses from the default of financial institutions or losses suffered in other asset classes such as mortgages. Last but not least, the test was only about solvency but not about liquidity. If some banks have mismatched maturities, i.e. they have borrowed short and lend long, they have to refinance their short term debts. If there are not enough savings available or no one is willing to refinance, illiquidity is the result. The illiquidity may then trigger solvency problems. The degree of maturity mismatch and the danger of illiquidity were, however, not considered in the tests. Thus, the assumptions were very restricted and seem to be chosen to get the desired result: all banks are sound except those that everyone knew before that they are unsound. Curiously, the Irish banks that a few months later were bailed out by the Irish governments passed the test.

Yet, for the moment , a total collapse of the system was averted and the Euro recovered some of its losses during the summer.

IRELAND

The sovereign debt crisis returned with full swing after summer vacations. On August 25 Ireland was downgraded by S&P to AA– which was still one level better than Italy. S&P expected Ireland's debt to rise to 113 percent of GDP in 2012. The estimate for the recapitalization of the banking system was raised from €35 billion to €59 billion. In September, the pressure on the yields of peripheral countries continued to intensify in response to the problems of the Anglo Irish Bank and the costs its recapitalization implied for the Irish government.

Around the same time plans of the German government were published that aimed at strengthening the sanctions of the SGP. Schäuble suggested to withhold EU infrastructure subsidies from countries violating the SGP and to reduce their voting rights. The Spanish government protested against such a reform. The struggle between fiscally more responsible and less responsible government continued.

The European banking system was close to collapse again in mid September 2010 as investors feared that Ireland could not stem the recapitalization of its banking sector. On September 17 the cost of insuring Irish debt rose to record levels and the Irish stock market plunged. The panic was contained only when the ECB bought Irish bonds signaling that it was willing to support the Irish government in the same way it did with Greece and other peripheral governments. In contrast to the spring panic, the crisis was contained because markets knew that the ECB stood there to buy up all bonds necessary and was accompanied by a €750 billion rescue fund.

With peripheral bonds on its balance sheet, the ECB continued to lose its independence. The ECB must help to prevent losses in these bonds through further support to these countries. The ECB becomes hostage of irresponsible politicians to pay their bill. As a consequence to impending losses resulting from its bond purchases, in December 2010 the ECB got a €5 billion capital boost. The increase in capital reduced the profits paid out to the EMU governments.

After pressures had calmed down following the bond purchases of the ECB, a summit in Brussels on October 29 showed again the power of the German government resulting from underwriting the debts of peripheral governments. The rescue fund had a limited term of three years. At the end of October, German chancellor Angela Merkel made it clear that the term would be extended only if there was a reform which would make private holders of government debt participate in the costs of future sovereign bailouts. In other words, Germany threatened to take away part of the explicit bailout guarantee it gave to private investors in government debts. Investors could suffer losses in bailouts after 2013. As a consequence of this move, investors started selling government bonds of PIIGS countries. Yields increased.

The market's attention focused on Ireland again. The Irish government had an estimated deficit of an unbelievable 32.5 percent of GDP for 2010 and its total government debt stood at 80 percent of GDP after repeated spending to prop up its insolvent banking system.

While the deficit is huge, the Irish problems are somewhat different than the fiscal problems of other PIIGS governments. Other PIIGS governments suffer from high and structural public deficits due to unsustainable welfare spending and uncompetitive factor markets. Governments, most prominently the Greek one, used deficit spending to artificially increase the living standards of their populations. Deficits financed the unemployed, public employees, and pensioners; this served to sustain inflexible labor markets.

In Ireland the problems were somewhat different. While Ireland also had an important and costly welfare state, in some sense Ireland was even too competitive. Ireland has the lowest corporate tax rate in the Economic and Monetary Union (at 12.5 percent). The tax rate attracted banks from all over the world to expand their businesses on the island. As a consequence, Ireland's banking sector expanded substantially. During the boom years, banks earned immense profits through their privilege of credit expansion and their implicit government backing. As a result of the credit expansion, an Irish housing bubble developed. And its burst caused substantial losses and even insolvency for Irish banks.

While banking profits during the boom were private, its losses were socialized on September 30, 2008, when the Irish government guaranteed all Irish bank liabilities. As of late 2010, Ireland had injected about €50 billion into its banking system. The Irish problems were created, not only by an excessive welfare system, but also by the socialization of the losses of a privileged banking system.

The Irish bailout costs €85 billion at a subsidized 5.8 percent interest rate. Part of it could be used to set up a fund for the Irish banking system. The bailout made ordinary taxpayers responsible for loans that serve to cover bank losses, and the Irish population largely opposed it. The Irish understood that the bailout money will mainly serve, not to sustain the living standards of public employees, the unemployed, or pensioners (as in the Greek case), but rather to sustain the living standards of bankers.

Due to the opposition, the Irish government decided not to have general elections before the budget was passed. The budget included an increase of the sales tax from 21 percent to 23 percent. Effectively, the Irish population was forced to assume the debts of banks and then pay them back over the years. No democratic vote on the bailout was allowed because the Irish would most certainly vote it down.

Why did the Eurozone governments pressure Ireland to ask for the bailout?

First, yields on bonds of PIIGS countries were rising. After the announcement of Merkel's reform plans, market participants started to fear that they would suffer losses from PIIGS bonds. Eurozone governments believed that by bailing out Ireland and showing determination they would take pressure of Portugal. Portugal—with structural problems similar to those of Greece—is important because Spanish banks have invested important sums in Portugal. If Portugal were to fall, the Spanish banking system would fall along with it. At this point, the rescue fund would have been empty and the situation uncontrollable. In order to stop this chain reaction, Ireland was pressured to accept the bailout.

Second, it was important to bail out Irish banks because English, French, and German banks had invested important sums in Ireland. Irish losses could eat up the capital of European banks and bring down the whole European banking system and its government allies.

But how could the Irish government be "convinced" to accept a bailout even though the Irish population was strongly opposed to it? Why would the Irish government ask for a bailout even though it claimed to be funded until well into 2011? There were two instruments to pressure the Irish government.

The first is the financing that Irish banks receive from the European Central Bank (ECB). Since the financial crisis, Irish banks have depended on loans from the ECB. Without these loans, the Irish banks would go bankrupt, implying tremendous losses for the Irish government, which guaranteed its banks' loans. Indeed, Trichet mentioned during the days in which the Irish government was still resisting a bailout that the ECB was not willing to extend the emergency loans to Irish banks forever. The second instrument was Germany's threat of withdrawing from its guarantees. Once Germany takes away its guarantees for overindebted governments in the Eurozone, these governments are sure to fail due to soaring interest rates. Thus Germany can pressure peripheral countries to make reforms or accept bailouts.

The Irish bailout failed to stop the chain reaction. Portuguese and Spanish yields continued to climb. When someone gets bailed out, someone has to pay for it. Governments of the Eurozone have to pay higher interest rates for their own debts due to the additional burden caused by the loans to Ireland. Indeed, the yields of even German government bonds increased after the bailout.

The Irish bailout fastened the trend toward the centralization of power in the European Union. European politicians already indirectly determine the Irish budget. For instance, they repeatedly told the Irish government to increase taxes, such as the sales tax.

They also put tremendous pressure on the Irish government to abandon its policy of a low corporate-tax rate, a policy that many European politicians regard as "fiscal dumping." Here, at last, the Irish government resisted.

AXEL WEBER

The two most important events of winter and spring 2011 were Merkel's idea for a Pact for Competitiveness in exchange for an extension of the rescue fund and Axel Weber's resigning as a candidate for the President of the ECB. In February, Axel Weber announced that he was to step down as President of the Bundesbank on April 30 which would rule him out as the next President of the ECB. Many people had considered the conservative Bundesbanker Weber as the next choice for the ECB's presidency and put much hope in him. Why did he step down? Weber had criticized the politics of the ECB several times. Starting with his critique of the ECB's quantitative easing by buying covered bonds, he repeatedly had criticized the purchase of government bonds to prop up insolvent governments. Weber had always pushed for a more restrictive monetary policy without finding a majority for his opinion. He had not been supported strongly as a candidate by Merkel who wanted political concessions from Sarkozy, a strong opponent of Weber.

The most likely explanation for Weber's exit is that he feared inflation and did not want to be responsible for gigantic bailouts and high inflation. Weber himself spoke of "lacking acceptance" of his anti-inflationary views as a reason for his exit. Possibly Weber was even pressured to resign. The Council of the European Union (the Council of Ministers) decides with a qualified majority on the next president of the ECB. France and Italy can prevent with their votes any candidate. Thus, it is possible that Weber was convinced to resign "voluntarily" to prevent an éclat.[20]

---

[20] See Roland Vaubel, "Eine andere Interpretation des Weber Rücktritts," 2011, http://wirtschaftlichefreiheit.de/

European monetary policy is no longer made by the Bundesbank. Followers of this tradition are simply outvoted. Thus, the German ex-finance minister Peer Steinbrück said that he did not want to become President of the ECB when he was proposed as a candidate. His explanation was revealing. He stated that he would be in the minority as he had similar policy views as Weber.

THE PACT FOR COMPETITIVENESS
AND THE EXTENSION OF THE RESCUE FUND

The Pact for Competitiveness (later renamed into Europlus pact) may stand symbolic for the epic failure of Merkel's bargaining. The events of May 2010 installed a €750 billion rescue fund with Germany and other solvent countries underwriting it. Yet, the rescue fund was limited for three years, meaning that in 2013 Germany would not have to bailout peripheral governments; an important ace in the hole.

Merkel used the ace to demand automatic sanctions in a reformed SGP, the loss of voting rights for countries violating the SGP and losses for private investors in restructurings of public debts. She and her government opposed an extension of the bailout fund as well as Eurobonds proposed by the President of Luxembourg Jean-Claude Juncker, as well as Italian, Portuguese and Greek politicians. On October 27 2010 Merkel still had pronounced the following about the rescue fund: "It [the fund] ends 2013. This is what we wanted and enacted. There cannot be and will not be a simple extension of the fund, because it does not serve as a long term instrument, because it sends to markets and member governments wrong signals and causes dangerous expectations. It causes the expectation that Germany and other member states and thereby also taxpayers of these countries in the case of a crisis will somehow fill in and could assume the risk of investors."[21]

---

[21] Quoted in Frank Schäffler, "Europäischer Stabilitätsmechanismus (ESM)," 2011, *Schriftliche Erklärung*, www.frank-schaeffler.de.

Curiously, and despite Merkel's position, on December 16, the European Council agreed on a permanent rescue fund. This was a great defeat for the German position, who always insisted and maintained that it would only be until 2013.

As an exchange for the extension of the rescue fund Merkel insisted on a "pact for competitiveness." Her initial proposal included fiscal harmonization (with a range for tax rates), harmonization of retirement age (70) and wages settings (eliminating inflation-indexed wages), limits for debts and deficits, a debt brake (similar to the German one), ex-ante budget control by Brussels, and sanctions for countries that does not fulfil these rules. While some steps go in the right direction, like the reduction of public pensions, no inflation indexed wages and deficit controls, the plan establishes a dangerous centralization. Sarkozy supported Merkel as her plan was a step toward the economic government that the French government had always wanted. Moreover, in the smaller Euro group as opposed to the EU 27, France and its allies had more weight against Germany. Trichet regarded a United States of Europe as possible, which he saw as "our historical project."

The events were a total defeat for German taxpayers. Not only did they underwrite a permanent rescue fund, but the French government got also its long desired economic government. Even though in the beginning there may be a strong German influence, in the long term its influence will be reduced, as has been the case of the ECB where Germany gets outvoted. At the same time Merkel gave up her demand for an automatic participation of private investors in bailouts.

In the short run, one may find some positive aspects of the determination of fiscal policies by Brussels or indirectly by Germany. When Germany or Brussels tells Spain, Greece, or Ireland to reduce their deficits or privatize their public pension systems, the result for people living in these countries may be a reduced size of the government in the short run. But such centralization of power in the EU will likely prove to be disastrous for liberty in the long run. One factor that frequently hampers governments' attempts to increase their power via increases in taxation or regulation is the competition of other governments. If taxes get too high in a country, economic agents will flee to countries with lower tax rates (such as Ireland, with its low corporate tax rate). If economic policy is centralized in the European Union, this limitation on government power is eliminated. European politicians already aim at a harmonization of fiscal policies and talk about benchmarks for tax rates. Once fiscal policies are harmonized, there will be a tendency toward an increase of power in Brussels and then toward an increase of tax rates throughout the Eurozone. The bailouts, the permanent rescue fund, and the economic government may save the Euro in the short run, but at the cost of building a strong, central European state, as national policymaking is transferred to Brussels in exchange for bailouts. The turmoil produced by the Euro will then have served as an instrument for the development of a centralized state in Europe.

On March 11, in an EU summit, the transfer union took further shape. The rescue fund was extended and will allow for primary market purchases of government bonds. Countries like Portugal may issue bonds which are then bought by the rescue fund. The rescue fund issues bonds to finance these purchases; a procedure that amounts to Euro bonds through the back door. Taxpayers from solvent countries purchase the debts of struggling governments. Germany might guarantee for about €200 billion instead for €123 billion before. The EFSF had an amount of €440 billion of which only €250 billion got an AAA rating. The new permanent European Stability Mechanism (ESM) that starts in 2013 will have an effective capacity of €500billion and may purchase bonds directly from governments at their nominal value. The ESM will get €80 billion in cash, €22 billion from Germany. The cash payment imply €600–900 million interest costs for Germany per year. The capital of the ESM is supposed to be €700 billion in order to guarantee the issuance of €500 billion AAA– rated loans. Germany will bear 27.1 percent of the total costs. Hans Werner Sinn estimated the total burden of the bailouts and the rescue fund to be €366 billion for Germany.[22]

If governments are insolvent, arbitrary distinguished from illiquid, private investors will participate in a haircut and suffer losses. The most probable outcome is that governments will always be considered just to be illiquid and private investors will never suffer losses.

What did Merkel get in return? The Pact for Competitiveness remained vague. Sanctions for violating governments were not mentioned. At least, Merkel maintained a veto for future loans to struggling countries as bailouts must be unanimous, which she tried to sell as a great victory.

The summit brought also a hidden debt restructuring for Greece. It was agreed to lower Greece's interest rates from 5.2 percent to 4.2 percent. The repayment period of Greek loans was extended to seven and a half years from three years. This implies a partial restructuring and important interest losses for taxpayers from solvent nations. Curiously, the Irish loans at 5.8 percent were not lowered because the new Irish Prime Minister Enda Kenny did not agree to raise corporate taxes in return.

On the next summit on March 24 and 25, the changes from March 11 were finally approved. Even though on March 23 Portuguese President Socrates resigned after his latest austerity package was not approved by the parliament, Portugal still did not want to tap the rescue fund.

PORTUGAL

The collapse of Portuguese public finances were only a matter of time.

In the beginning of January 2011, as pressure mounted, an important Portuguese bonds auction went well. The government paid less than the 7 percent for 10 year bonds deemed

---

[22] Hans Werner Sinn, "Deutschland: Die Lotsen gehen von Board," 2011, www.mmnews.de.

unsustainable by several Portuguese parliamentarians.[23] Bond purchased of the ECB in the days before supported the auction. The ECB bailed out Portugal. Barclays Capital estimated that the ECB bought €19.5 billion of the €21.7 billion Portuguese bonds sold in 2010. From February 2011 on the bond yield was consistently above 7 percent, rising to 8.5 percent by April. Public debts were at 92 percent of GDP in 2010. The public deficit in 2010 was at 8.6 percent down from 10 percent in 2009. The austerity measures that met strong resistance on the street were only able to lower the deficit by 1.4 percentage points.

Portugal's case is similar to the Greek one. The economy is uncompetitive, with a huge public sector and inflexible factor markets. The structure of the economy is not aligned with consumer wishes and maintained artificially by government spending.

During the first decade of the twenty-first century, public and private sectors increased their indebtedness. Interest rates were artificially low due to the credit expansion initiated by the Eurosystem and the implicit underwriting of Portuguese debts by Germany. The Iberian country lived beyond its means, increasing its public sector to 50 percent of GDP in 2009 under a huge fiscal pressure. The trade deficit reached 10 percent of GDP.

An artificially high standard of living was made possible by the accumulation of debts at artificially low interest rates. The necessary adjustment of the backward economy was delayed by artificially low credits. Between 2002 and 2007 the Portuguese GDP grew only 6 percent, while Spain grew 22 percent (housing bubble), Ireland 37 percent (banking bubble) and Greece 27 percent (public sector bubble). Portuguese unemployment doubled from 4 percent to 8, percent while the Spanish, Irish or Greek unemployment did not grow or even fell. Tax revenues increased

---

[23] Alexander Liddington-Cox, "THE DAILY CHART: Portugal's Austerity Impasse," *BusinessSpectator* (March 23, 2011), http://www.businessspectator.com.au.

by 35 percent in Portugal, but by 50 percent in Greece and 70 percent in Spain and Ireland.[24]

While countries such as Germany started structural reforms, reduced public social spending, reduced real wages, Portugal did use cheap credit to delay a reform of its productive model. Other peripheral countries used the cheap credits to build bubbles.

With rising interest rates and rising debts and no serious reforms, the country was going to default sooner or later if it was not bailed out. The Portuguese economy owes €80 billion to Spanish banks. If there is a default of the Portuguese government, many companies depending on the vast public sector will follow suit and be unable to pay their debts to the Spanish banks which in turn triggers a Spanish banking crisis and rising yield for Spanish government bonds. Unsurprisingly, the Portuguese government agreed to a bailout amounting to €78 billion on May 3 2011, after the ECB and the Commission had used similar threats and pressures as they did in the case of Ireland.

Thus, expectations remain grim. The European Union has become a transfer union. Interest rates that most governments have to pay on their debts remain at a high level. Sovereign debt levels are still on the rise. The future will tell us if the situation was sustainable.

---

[24] See Juan Ramón Rallo, "Portugal: Una decada (mal)viviendo del crédito barato," *juanramonrallo.com* (March 23, 2011), http://www.juanramonrallo.com, and Juan Ramón Rallo, "España sí es Portugal," *juanramonrallo.com* (March 29, 2011), http://www.juanramonrallo.com.

CHAPTER ELEVEN

The Future of the Euro

Have we already reached the point of no return? Can the sovereign debt crisis be contained and the financial system stabilized? Can the Euro be saved? In order to answer these questions we must take a look at the sovereign debt crisis, whose advent was largely the result of government interventions in response to the financial crisis.

As Austrian business cycle theory explains, the credit expansion of the fractional-reserve banking system caused an unsustainable boom. At artificially low interest rates, additional investment projects were undertaken even though there was no corresponding increase in real savings. The investments were simply paid by new paper credit. Many of these investments projects constituted malinvestments that had to be liquidated sooner or later. In the present cycle, these malinvestments occurred mainly in the overextended automotive, housing, and financial sectors.

The liquidation of malinvestments is beneficial in the sense that it purges inefficient projects and realigns the structure of production according to consumer preferences. Factors of production that are misused in malinvestments are liberated and transferred to projects that consumers want realized more urgently.

Along with the unsustainable credit-induced boom, indebtedness in society increases. Credit expansion and its artificially low interest rates allow for a debt level that would not be possible in a one hundred percent commodity standard. Debts increase beyond the level real resources warrant because interest rates on the debts are low, and because new debts may be created out of thin air to substitute for old ones. The fractional reserve banking system causes an over-indebtedness of both private citizens and governments.

While the boom and over-indebtedness occurred on a world-wide scale, the European boom had its own signature ingredients. Because of the introduction of the Euro, interest rates fell in the high inflationary countries even though savings did not increase. The result was a boom for Southern countries and Ireland.

Implicit support on the part of the German government toward members of the monetary union reduced interest rates (their risk component) for both private and public debtors artificially. The traditionally high inflation countries saw their debt burden reduced and, in turn, a spur in private and public consumption spending. The relatively high exchange rates fixed forever in the Euro benefitted high inflation countries as well. Durable consumer goods such as cars or houses were bought, leading to housing booms, the most spectacular of which was in Spain. Southern countries lost competitiveness as wage rates kept increasing. Overconsumption and the loss in competitiveness were sustained for several years by ever higher private and public debts and the inflow of new money created by the banking system.

The European boom affected countries in unique ways. Malinvestments and over-consumption were higher in the high inflation countries and lower in Northern countries, such as Germany, where savings rates had remained higher.

The scheme fell apart when the worldwide boom came to its inevitable end. The liquidation of malinvestments—falling housing prices and bad loans—caused problems in the banking system. Defaults and investment losses threatened the solvency of banks, including European banks. Solvency problems triggered a liquidity crisis in which maturity-mismatched banks had difficulties rolling over their short-term debt.

At the time, alternatives were available that would have tackled the solvency problem and recapitalized the banking system.[1] Private investors could have injected capital into the banks that they deemed viable in the long run. In addition, creditors could have been transformed into equity holders, thereby reducing the banks' debt obligations and bolstering their equity. Unsustainable financial institutions—for which insufficient private capital or creditors-turned-equity-holders were found—would have been liquidated.

Yet the available free-market solutions to the banks' solvency problems were set aside, and another option was chosen. Governments all over the world injected capital into banks while guaranteeing the liabilities of the banking system. Since taxes are unpopular, these government injections were financed by the less-unpopular increases in public debt. In other words, the malinvestments induced by the inflationary-banking system found an ultimate sponsor—the government—in the form of ballooning public debts.

There are other reasons why public debts increased dramatically. Governments undertook additional measures to fight against the healthy purging of the economy, thereby delaying the recovery. In addition to the financial sector, other overextended industries received direct capital injections or benefited from government subsidies and spending programmes.

Two prime examples of subsidy recipients are the automotive sector in many European countries and the construction sector in Spain. Factor mobility was hampered by public works absorbing the scarce factors needed in other industries. Greater subsidies for the unemployed increased the deficit while reducing incentives to find work outside of the overextended industries. Another factor that added to the deficits was the diminished tax revenue caused by reduced employment and profits.

Government interventions not only delayed the recovery, but they delayed it at the cost of ballooning public deficits—increases

---

[1] See Philipp Bagus, "The Fed's Dilemma," *Mises.org daily* (October 8, 2009), http://mises.org.

which themselves add to preexisting, high levels of public debt. And preexisting public debt is an artifact of unsustainable welfare states. As the unfunded liabilities of public-pension systems pose virtually insurmountable obstacles to modern states, in one sense the crisis—with its dramatic increase in government debts—is a leap forward toward the inevitable collapse of the welfare state.

As we have already seen, there is an additional wrinkle in the debt problem in Europe. When the Euro was created, it was implicitly assumed among member nations that no nation would leave the Euro after joining it. If things went from bad to worse, a nation could be rescued by the rest of the EMU. A severe sovereign debt problem was preprogrammed with this implicit bailout guarantee.

The assumed support of fiscally stronger nations reduced interest rates for fiscally irresponsible nations artificially. These interest rates allowed for levels of debt not justified by the actual situation of a given country. Access to cheap credit allowed countries like Greece to maintain a gigantic public sector and ignore the structural problem of uncompetitive wage rates. Any deficits could be financed by money creation on the part of the ECB, externalising the costs to fellow EMU members.

From a politician's point of view, incentives in such a system are explosive: "If I, as a campaigning politician, promise gifts to my voters in order to win the election, I can externalize the cost of those promises to the rest of the EMU through inflation—and future taxpayers have to pay the debt. Even if the government needs a bailout (a worst-case scenario), it will happen only in the distant, post-election future.

Moreover, when the crisis occurs, I will be able to convince voters that I did not cause the crisis. It just fell upon the country in the form of a natural disaster. Or better still, it is the doing of evil speculators. While austerity measures, imposed by the EMU or IMF, loom in the future, the next election is just around the corner."

It is easy to see how the typical shortsightedness of demo-cratic politicians combines well with the possibility of

externalizing deficit costs to other nations, resulting in explosive debt inflation.

Amid the circumstances such as these, European states
were of course already well on their way to bankruptcy due to
unsustainable welfare states when the financial crisis hit and
deficits exploded. Markets became distrustful of government
promises. The Greek episode is an obvious example of such
distrust. Because politicians want to save the Euro experiment
at all costs, the bailout guarantee has become explicit. Greece
receives loans from the EMU and the IMF, totaling an estimated
€110 billion from 2010 to 2012. In addition, even though Greek
government bonds are rated as junk, the ECB continues to accept
them and has even started to buy them outright.[2]

Contagions from Greece also threaten other countries that
have extraordinarily high deficits or debts, such as Spain and
Italy. Some of these suffer from high unemployment and inflexible labor markets. A spread to these countries could trigger
their insolvency—and the end of the Euro. The EMU has reacted
to possibility of danger and has gone "all out," pledging, along
with the IMF, an additional €750 billion support package for
troubled member states. Ireland was already forced to tap the
rescue fund in November 2010. Portugal in May 2011.

CAN GOVERNMENTS CONTAIN THE CRISIS?

The Greek government has tried several ways to end its debt
problem. It has announced a freeze on public salaries, a reduction
in the number of public servants, and an increase in taxes on gas,
tobacco, alcohol, and big real-estate properties.

But are these measures sufficient? There are mainly six ways
out of the debt problems for overly indebted countries in the
EMU.

---

[2] See Robert Lindsay, "ECB in U-turn on Junk Bonds to Save Greek Banking
System," *Times Online* (May 4, 2010), http://business.timesonline.co.uk. On January 14 2011 Fitch was the last of the three big rating agencies that downgraded Greek government debt to junk.

Overly indebted countries can reduce public spending. The Greek government has been reducing its spending but still runs deficits. The reduction in spending may simply not be enough. In fact, the Greek government failed to meet its goal to reduce its deficit to 8.1 percent in 2010. Despite the government's promise to substantially reduce its deficit and to bring it below 3 percent in 2014, the Greek deficit in 2010 was 10.5 percent of GDP and is predicted to be 9.5 percent in 2011. Additional €60 billion loans to bring the Greek government through 2013 started to be discussed in May 2011. Moreover, it is not clear if the government can stick to these small spending cuts. Greece is famous for its riots in reaction to relatively minor political reforms. As the majority of the population seems to be against spending cuts, the government may not be able to reduce spending sufficiently and lastingly.

Countries can increase their competitiveness to boost tax income. The Greek government, however, has lacked the courage to pursue this course. Its huge public sector has not been substantially reduced, and wage rates remain uncompetitive as a result of strong and still privileged labor unions. This lack of competitiveness is a permanent drag on public finances. An artificially high standard of living is maintained via government deficits. Workers who are uncompetitive at high wage rates find employment in the public sector, drop out into earlier retirement, or receive unemployment benefits.

The alternative would be to stop subsidising unemployment, be it in the disguised form of early retirement, unproductive government jobs, or openly, with unemployment benefits. This would bring down wages in the private economy. The abolition of labor union privileges would further drag down prices. Competitiveness of Greek companies would thereby increase and government deficits would be reduced. Other Latin countries are faced with similar situations.

Governments can reduce debts by selling public property. Government may reduce debts by the one-time measure of privatising public property. Indeed, the Greek government was pressured to do so and even to sell public islands. The Greek government resisted to sell islands or monuments out of national pride. It resisted selling public companies because their new private owners would have drastically reduced the overblown workforce, leading to strong resistance on the streets. After complaints by the Commission and the IMF, in May 2011 the Greek government committed to privatizations of an unrealistic €50 billion.

Countries can try to increase their revenues by increasing taxes. Greece has done this. But the increase in taxes is causing new problems for Greeks. Wealth is being re-channelled from the productive private sector into the unproductive public sector. The incentives to be productive, to save and invest are further reduced. Growth is hampered.

Growth induced by deregulation. This way may be the easiest change to achieve politically, and the most promising. Its disadvantage is that it takes time that some countries may not have.

With sufficient growth, tax revenues increase and reduce deficits automatically. Growth and innovation is generated by an overall liberalization of the troubled economies. With regulations and privileges abolished, and public property and companies privatized, new areas are opened to competing entrepreneurs. The private sector has more room to breathe.

The packages enacted by the Greek government consist of this kind of deregulation. Greece has eliminated privileges—like mandatory licenses for truck drivers (who unsurprisingly went on strike and paralysed the country for some days). But Greece has, at the same time, taken measures making it more difficult for the private sector to breathe. Tax increases, and especially the increases of the sales tax, are good examples. The measures seem to be insufficient to produce the economic boom necessary to reduce public debts.

External help. But can an external bailout do what insufficient liberalization cannot? Can the €110 billion bailout of the Greek government, combined with the €750 billion of additional, promised support, stop the sovereign debt crisis, or have we come to the point of no return? There are several reasons why pouring good money after bad may be incapable of stopping the spread of the sovereign debt crisis.

1. The €110 billion granted to Greece may itself not be enough. What happens if Greece has not managed to reduce its deficits sufficiently at the end of their term? The Greek government does not seem to be on the path to becoming self-sufficient. A default of some kind seems to be inevitable. The Greek government is doing, paradoxically, both too little and too much to achieve this. It is doing too much insofar as it is raising taxes, thereby hurting the private sector. At the same time, Greece is doing too little insofar as it is not sufficiently reducing its expenditures and deregulating its economy. In addition, strikes are damaging the economy and riots endanger austerity measures. The situation in Ireland and Portugal is not much better. The €85 billion granted to Ireland and the €78 billion granted to Portugal may not be enough to solve their public debt problems.

2. By spending money on Greece, Ireland, and Portugal, fewer funds are available for bailing out other countries. There exists a risk for some countries (such as Spain) that not enough money will be available to bail them out if needed. As a result, interest rates charged on their now-riskier bonds were pushed up. Although the additional €750 billion support package was installed in response to this risk, the imminent threat of contagion was stopped at the cost of what will likely be higher debts for the stronger EMU members, ultimately aggravating the sovereign debt problem even further.

3. Someone will eventually have to pay for the EMU loans to the Greek government at four percent (formerly five). (In fact, the United States is paying for part of this sum indirectly through its participation in the IMF).[3] As the debts of the rest of the EMU members increase, they

---

[3] See Bob Davis, "Who's on the Hook for the Greek Bailout?" *The Wall Street Journal* (May 5, 2010), http://online.wsj.com.

will have to pay higher interest rates than they would otherwise. When the bailout was announced, Portugal was paying more for its debt already and would have lost outright by lending money at five percent interest to Greece.[4] As both the total debt and interest rates for the Portuguese government increased, it reached the point where the government was not able to refinance itself anymore. The Portuguese government was then bailed out by the rest of the EMU, which pushed up debts and interest rates for other countries still further. This could knock out the next weakest state, which would then need a bailout, and so on, in a domino effect.

4. The bailout of Greece, Ireland, and Portugal (and the promise of support for other troubled member states) has reduced incentives to manage deficits. The rest of the EMU may well think that they, like Greece, have a right to the EMU's support. For example, since interest rates may stabilize following the bailout, pressure is artificially removed from the Spanish government to reduce its deficit and make labor markets more flexible — measures that are needed but are unpopular with voters.

Spain is the next government in line after Portugal. Spain's problems are many fold and contain characteristics of other peripheral countries. The main problem is Spain's high public and private indebtedness. Artificially low interest rates caused by the ECB allowed for a housing boom. Housing prices soared, Spaniards indebted themselves and lived beyond their means. As housing prices fall and Spaniards lose their jobs many cannot pay their debts. Constructors and private households default posing problems to the banking system.

Public debts almost doubled from 36.1 percent in 2007 to an estimated 70.2 percent in 2011. Private debts are at over 200 percent of GDP. From a housing boom induced surplus of 1.7

---

[4] It is unclear whether countries that pay higher interest rates than five percent will participate. Tagesschau, "Müss Deutschland noch mehr zahlen?" *Tagesschau* (May 6, 2010), http://www.tagesschau.de.

percent in 2007 the public deficit exploded to 11.2 percent in 2009 and 9.3 percent in 2010. The unemployment rate hovers around 20 percent. At the same time politicians do not seem willing to engage in structural reforms.

Spanish banks may still have important bad loans and are exposed heavily to Portugal. Higher interest rates as announced by the ECB to curb inflation will pose problems to public finances and may trigger more private defaults and increase problems for the banking system.

The next countries in line are Italy and Belgium which are too big to be bailed out by the existing rescue fund. In 2010 Italy's public debts rose to 119 percent of GDP with a deficit of 4.6 percent. Belgium, who does not have a functioning government, has public debt around 100 percent of GDP. The final nail in the coffin of the EMU, however, may be France. France debt to GDP ratio rose to 81.7 percent, with a deficit of 7 percent. Even small structural reforms such as an increase in retirement age from 60 to 62 years triggered massive protests and strikes in October 2010 which raises doubts on the political possibility to substantially reduce France's deficit.

While deficits have been reduced somewhat, public debts are still rising all over Europe, in some countries fast and unsustainable. With every day that debts continue to rise and severe structural reforms are not undertaken, it is more likely that we have passed the point of no return.

Conclusion

The institutional setup of the EMU has been an economic disaster. The Euro is a political project; political interests have brought the European currency forwards on its grievous way and have been clashing over it as a result. And economic arguments launched to disguise the true agenda behind the Euro have failed to convince the general population of its advantages.

The Euro has succeeded in serving as a vehicle for centralization in Europe and for the French government's goal of establishing a European Empire under its control—curbing the influence of the German state. Monetary policy was the political means toward political union. Proponents of a socialist Europe saw the Euro as their trump against the defence of a classical liberal Europe that had been expanding in power and influence ever since the Berlin Wall came down. The single currency was seen as a step toward political integration and centralization. The logic of interventions propelled the Eurosystem toward a political unification under a central state in Brussels. As national states are abolished, the market place of Europe becomes a new Soviet Union.

Could the central state save political elites all over Europe? By merging monetarily with financially stronger governments, they were able to retain their power and the confidence of the markets. Financially stronger governments opposed to abrupt changes and recessions were forced help out. The alternative was too grim.

Mediterranean countries and particular the French government had another interest in the introduction of the Euro. The Bundesbank had traditionally pursued a sounder monetary policy than other central banks, and had served as an embarrassing standard of comparison and indirectly dictated monetary policy in Europe. If a central bank did not follow the Bundesbank's restrictive policy, its currency would have to devalue and realign. Some French politicians regarded the influence of the Bundesbank as an unjustified and unacceptable power in the control of the militarily defeated Germany.

French politicians wanted to create a common central bank to control the German influence. They envisioned a central bank that would cooperate in the political goals. The purchase of Greek government bonds from French banks by an ECB led by Trichet is the outcome—and a sign of the strategy's victory.

The German government gave in for several reasons. The single currency was seen by many as the price for reunification. The German ruling class benefited from the stabilization of the financial and sovereign system. The harmonization of technological and social standards that came with European integration was a benefit to technologically advanced German companies and their socially cared-for workers. German exporters benefited from a currency that was weaker than the Deutschmark would have been.

But German consumers lost out. Before the introduction of the Euro, a less inflationary Deutschmark, increases in productivity, and exports had caused the Deutschmark to appreciate against other currencies after World War II. Imports and vacations became less expensive, raising the standard of living of most Germans.

Sometimes it is argued that a single currency cannot work across countries with different institutions and cultures. It is true that the fiscal and industrial structures of the EMU countries vary greatly. They have experienced different rates of price inflation in the past. Productivity, competitiveness, standards of living, and market flexibility differ. But these differences must not hinder the functioning of a single currency. In fact, there are very different structures within countries such as Germany, as well. Rural Bavaria is quite different in its structure from coastal Bremen. Even within cities or households, individuals are quite heterogeneous in their use of the same currency.

Moreover, under the gold standard, countries worldwide enjoyed a single currency. Goods traded internationally between rich and poor countries. The gold standard did not break down because participating countries had different structures. It was destroyed by governments who wanted to get rid of binding, golden chains and increase their own spending.

The Euro is not a failure because participating countries have different structures, but rather because it allows for redistribution in favor of countries whose banking systems and governments inflate the money supply faster than others. By deficit spending and printing government bonds, governments can indirectly create money. Government bonds are bought by the banking system. The ECB accepts the bonds as collateral for new loans. Governments convert bonds into new money. Countries that have higher deficits than others can maintain trade deficits and buy goods from exporting states with more balanced budgets.

The process resembles a tragedy of the commons. A country benefits from the redistribution process if it inflates faster than other countries do, i.e., if it has higher deficits than others. The incentives create a race to the printing press. The SGP has been found impotent to completely eliminate this race; the Euro system tends toward self explosion.

Government deficits cause a continuous loss in competitiveness of the deficit countries. Countries such as Greece can afford a welfare state, public employees, and unemployment at a higher standard of living than would have been possible without such high deficits. The deficit countries can import more goods than they export, paying the difference partly with newly printed government bonds.

Before the introduction of the Euro, these countries devalued their currencies from time to time in order to regain competitiveness. Now they do not need to devalue because government spending takes care of the resulting problems. Overconsumption spurred by reduced interest rates and nominal wage increases pushed for by labor unions increase the competitive disadvantage.

The system ran into trouble when the financial crisis accelerated deficit spending. The resulting sovereign debt crisis in Europe brings with it a centralization of power. The European Commission assumes more control over government spending and the ECB assumes powers such as the purchase of government bonds.

We have reached what may be called transfer union III. Transfer union I is direct redistribution via monetary payments managed by Brussels. Transfer union II is monetary redistribution chanelled through the ECB lending operations. Transfer union III brings out direct purchases of government bonds and bailout guarantees for over-indebted governments.

What will the future bring for a system whose incentives destine it for self-destruction?

1. The system may break up. A country might exit the EMU because it becomes advantageous to devalue its currency and default on its obligations. The government may simply not be willing to reduce government spending and remain in the EMU. Other countries may levy sanctions on a deficit country or stop to support it.

Alternatively, a sounder government such as Germany may decide to exit the EMU and return to the Deutschmark. German trade surpluses and less inflationary policy would likely lead to an appreciation of the new Deutschmark. The appreciation would allow for cheaper imports, vacations and investments abroad, and increased standard of living. The Euro might lose credibility and collapse. While this option is imaginable, the political will—for now—is still to stick by the Euro project.

2. The SGP will be reformed and finally enforced. Austerity measures and structural reforms in deficit countries lead to real economic growth and eliminate the deficit. A one-time haircut on bonds of highly indebted countries may reduce the existing debt burden.[1] Harsh and automatic penalties are enacted

---

[1] A (partial) default of a government would not necessarily imply an exit from the Eurozone. However, a partial default could trigger a European banking crisis and also the sell-off of bonds of other governments. The higher interest

if the three percent limit is infringed upon. Penalties may consist in a suspension of voting rights and EU subsidies, or in outright payments. But there are incentives for politicians to exceed the limit, making this scenario quite unlikely. The members of the EMU are still sovereign states, and the political class may not want to impose such harsh limits that diminish their power.

3. Incentives toward having higher deficits than the other countries will lead to a pronounced transfer union. Richer states pay to the poorer to cover deficits, and the ECB monetizes government debts. This development may lead to protests of richer countries and ultimately to their exit, as mentioned above. Another possible end of the transfer union is hyperinflation caused by a run on the printing press.

In the current crisis, governments seem to be hovering between options two and three. Which scenario will play out in the end is anyone's guess.

----

payments on bonds would most probably trigger these governments' downfalls. As the situation might get out of control, governments have tried to prevent such a situation and resisted haircuts so far. Moreover, a default alone would not be sufficient to substantially reduce the deficit in most countries. Interest payments on existing debts make up only the smaller part of deficits. [Desmond Lachman (2010, 31) writes that "had Greece and Ireland successfully managed to halve their public debts through restructuring in 2009, they would have still been left with budget deficits of over 10 percent of GDP."] If governments want to get around austerity measures and structural reforms, they would have to leave the Eurozone in order to be able to inflate their way out of their deficit problems. The implied devaluation would impoverish the population of these countries immediately.

References

Baader, Roland. 1993. *Die Euro-Katastrophe. Für Europas Vielfalt—gegen Brüssels Einfalt*. Böblingen: Anita Tykve.

Bagus, Philipp. 2003. "Deflation—When Austrians Become Interventionists." *Quarterly Journal of Austrian Economics* 6 (4) 2003: pp. 19–35.

----------------. 2004. "La tragedia de los bienes comunales y la escuela austriaca: Hardin, Hoppe, Huerta de Soto y Mises." *Procesos de Mercado: Revista Europea de Economía Política* 1 (2): pp. 125–134

----------------. 2006. "Five Common Errors about Deflation." *Procesos de Mercado: Revista Europea de Economía Política* 3 (1): pp. 105–123.

----------------. 2009a. "The Quality of Money." *Quarterly Journal of Austrian Economics* 12 (4): pp. 41–64.

----------------. 2009b. "The Fed's Dilemma." *Mises.org daily*, October 8, 2009, http://mises.org.

----------------. 2010. "Austrian Business Cycle Theory: Are 100 Percent Reserves Sufficient to Prevent a Business Cycle?" *Libertarian Papers*, 2 (2).

----------------. 2011. "The Tragedy of the Euro." *The Independent Review* 15 (4).

Bagus, Philipp and David Howden. 2009a. "The Federal Reserve and Eurosystem's Balance Sheet Policies During the Subprime Crisis: A Comparative Analysis." *Romanian Economic and Business Review*, 4 (3): pp. 165–185.

----------------. 2009b. "Qualitative Easing in Support of a Tumbling Financial System: A Look at the Eurosystem's Recent Balance Sheet Policies." *Economic Affairs* 21 (4): pp. 283–300.

Bagus, Philipp and Markus Schiml. 2009. "New Modes of Monetary Policy: Qualitative Easing by the Fed." *Economic Affairs* 29 (2) 2009: pp. 46–49.

----------------. 2010. "A Cardiograph of the Dollar's Quality: Qualitative Easing and the Federal Reserve Balance Sheet During the Subprime Crisis." *Prague Economic Papers* 19 (3) 2010: pp. 195–217.

Balzli, Beat. 2010. "How Goldman Sachs Helped Greece to Mask its True Debt." *Spiegel online*, http://www.spiegel.de.

Bandulet, Bruno. 2010. *Die letzten Jahre des Euro. Ein Bericht über das Geld, das die Deutschen nicht wollten*. Rottenburg: Kopp Verlag.

Bank for International Settlements. 2010. "International Banking and Financial Markets Development." *BIS Quarterly Report.* June 2010.

Bayer, Tobias. 2010. "Hilfen für Hellas: Kehrtwende kratzt an Glaubwürdigkeit der EZB." *Financial Times Deutschland,* http://www.ftd.de.

Booker, Christophe and Richard North. 2005. *The Great Deception: Can the European Union Survive?* London: Continuum.

Browne, John. 2010. "Euro Fiasco Threatens the World." *Triblive.* July 18. http://www.pittsburghlive.com.

Buchanan, James and Gordon Tullock. 1962. *The Calculus of Consent. Logical Foundations of Constitutional Democracy.* Ann Arbor: University of Michigan Press.

Cash-online. 2010. "Forsa: Deutsche überwiegend gegen den Euro-Rettungsschirm." News from June 7. http://www.cash-online.de.

Cecchetti, Stephen G. and Róisín O'Sullivan. 2003. "The European Central Bank and the Federal Reserve." *Oxford Review of Economic Policy* 19 (1): pp. 30–43.

Center for Geoeconomic Studies. 2010. "Greek Debt Crisis – Apocalypse Later." *Council on Foreign Relations.* September 2. http://blogs.cfr.org.

Connolly, Bernard. 1995. *The Rotten Heart of Europe: The Dirty War for Europe's Money.* London: Faber and Faber.

Cullen, Angela and Rainer Buergin. 2010. "Schaeuble Denied Twice by Merkel Defies Doctors in Saving Euro." *Bloomberg,* July 21. http://noir.bloomberg.com.

Das Weisse Pferd. 1998. "Die Risiken des Euro sind unübersehbar (1)." *Das Weisse Pferd – Urchristliche Zeitung für Gesellschaft, Religion, Politik und Wirtschaft,* August, 1998. http://www.das-weisse-pferd.com.

Davis, Bob. 2010. "Who's on the Hook for the Greek Bailout?" *The Wall Street Journal,* May 5. http://online.wsj.com.

Dutchnews.nl. 2010. "Dutch are the Biggest EU Net Payers: PVV." January 14. http://www.dutchnews.nl.

ECB. 2008. *The Implementation of Monetary Policy in the Euro Area: General Documentation on Eurosystem Monetary Policy Instruments and Procedures.* November, 2008. http://www.ecb.int.

----------------. 2010. *Monthly Bulletin: June.* http://www.ecb.int.

Eigendorf, Jörg, Florian Hassel, Stefanie Bolzen, Jan Dams, Daniel Eckert, Florian Eder, Thomas Exner, Michael Fabricius, Martin Greive, Sebastian Jost, Tobias Kaiser, Christoph B. Schiltz, Andre Tauber, Gesche Wüpper and Holger Zschäpitz. 2010. "Chronologie des Scheiterns." *Welt.online,* May 16. http://www.welt.de.

Eichengreen, Barry. 1991. "Is Europe an Optimum Currency Area?" *NBER working paper series,* no. 3579. January.

Einecke, Helga and Martin Hesse. 2010. "Kurz vor der Apokalypse." *Süddeutsche Zeitung,* June 16. http://www.sueddeutsche.de.

Erhard, Ludwig (1962/88). "Planification – kein Modell für Europa," in: Karl Hohmann (ed.), *Ludwig Erhard. Gedanken aus fünf Jahrzehnten*. Düsseldorf: ECON, pp. 770–780.

Evans-Pritchard, Ambrose. 2010. "Axa Fears 'Fatal-flaw' Will Destroy Eurozone." *Telegraph.co.uk*. June 14. http://www.telegraph.co.uk.

Federal Reserve. 2005. "The Federal Reserve System: Purposes and Functions." 9th ed., http://www.federalreserve.gov.

Feldstein, Martin. 1997. "The Political Economy of the European Political and Monetary Union: Political Sources of an Economic Liability." *Journal of Economic Perspectives* 11 (24): pp. 23–42.

Foreman-Peck, James. 2004. "The UK and the Euro: Politics versus Economics in a Long-Run Perspective." In *The Price of the Euro*, Jonas Ljundberg, ed., pp. 97–120. New York: Palgrave MacMillan.

Frankfurter Allgemeine Zeitung. April 13, 1992.

----------------. June 1, 1996.

Gave, Charles. 2010. "Was the Demise of the USSR a Negative Event?" *Investorsinsight.com*, John Mauldin, ed. May 5. http://investorsinsight.com.

Ginsberg, Roy H. 2007. *Demystifying the European Union. The Enduring Logic of Regional Integration*. Plymouth, UK: Rowman & Littlefield.

Granitsas, Alkman and Paris Costas. 2010. "Greek and German Media Tangle over Crisis." *The Wall Street Journal*, February 24. http://online.wsj.com.

GRReporter. 2010. "The Social Tourism of Bankrupt Greece," July 12. http://www.grreporter.info.

Hankel, Wilhelm, Wilhelm Nölling, Karl A. Schachtschneider and Jochaim Starbatty. 2001. *Die Euro-Illusion. Warum Europa scheitern muß*. Hamburg: Rowohlt.

Hannan, Daniel. 2010. "Germans! Stop Being Ripped Off!" *Telegraph.co.uk*. March 27. http://blogs.telegraph.co.uk.

Hannich, Günter. 2010. *Die kommende Euro-Katastrophe. Ein Finanzsystem vor dem Bankrott?* München: Finanzbuch Verlag.

Hardin, Garrett. 1968. "The Tragedy of the Commons." *Science*, New Series 162 (3859): pp. 1243–1248.

Hayek, Friedrich A. von. 1976. *Denationalisation of Money: An Analysis of the Theory and Practice of Concurrent Currencies*. London: Institute of Economic Affairs.

Henkel, Hans-Olaf. 2010. *Rettet unser Geld! Deutschland wird ausverkauft—Wie der Euro-Betrug unseren Wohlstand gefährdet*. München: Heyne.

Higgs, Robert. 1987. *Crisis and Leviathan: Critical Episodes in the Growth of American Government*. Oxford: Oxford University Press.

Hoeren, D. and O. Santen. 2010. "Griechenland-Pleite: Warum zahlen wir ihre Luxus-Renten mit Milliarden-Hilfe?" *bild-online.de*. April 27. http://bild.de.

Homburg, Stefan. 1997. "Hat die Währungsunion Auswirkungen auf die Finanzpolitik?," in Franz-Ulrich Willeke, ed., *Die Zukunft der D-Mark. Eine Streitschrift zur Europäischen Währungsunion.* München: Olzog, pp. 93–108.

Hoppe, Hans-Hermann. 1990a. "Banking, Nation States, and International Politics: A Sociological Reconstruction of the Present Economic Order." *Review of Austrian Economics* 4 (1): pp. 55–87.

----------------. 1990b. *"Marxist and Austrian Class Analysis."* Journal of Libertarian Studies 9 (2): pp. 79–93.

----------------. 2001. *Democracy: The God that Failed.* Rutgers, N.J.: Transaction Publishers.

Hoppe, Hans-Hermann, Jörg Guido Hülsmann and Walter Block. 1998. "Against Fiduciary Media." *Quarterly Journal of Austrian Economics* 1 (1): pp. 19–50.

Hosking, Patrick. 2008. "France Seeks €300 bn. Rescue Fund for Europe." *Timesonline.* October 2. http://business.timesonline.co.uk.

Hülsmann, Guido. 1997. "Political Unification: A Generalized Progression Theorem." *Journal of Libertarian Studies* 13 (1): pp. 81–96.

Huerta de Soto, Jesús. 2005. "Por una Europa libre." In *Nuevos Estudios de Economía Política,* pp. 214–216.

----------------. [2006] 2009. *Money, Bank Credit and Economic Cycles.* 2nd ed. Auburn, Ala.: Ludwig von Mises Institute.

Hutchison, Michael M. and Kenneth M. Kletzer. 1995. "Fiscal Convergence Criteria, Factor Mobility, and Credibility in Transition to Monetary Union in Europe." In *Monetary and Fiscal Policy in an Integrated Europe,* Barry Eichengreen, Jeffry Frieden and Jürgen von Hagen, eds. Berlin, Heidelberg: Springer.

Illmer, Andreas. 2010. "Merkel Rules Out German Bailout for Greece." *Deutsche Welle.* March 1. http://www.dw-world.de.

Irish Independent. 1959. "Catholicism Growing Strong in Europe," October 28, 1959.

Jones, Marc. 2010. "EU Will Accept Even Junk-rated Greek Bonds." *Reuters.* May 3. http://in.reuters.com.

Jonung, Lars and Eoin Drea. 2010. "It Can't Happen, It's a Bad Idea, It Won't Last: U.S. Economists on the EMU and the Euro, 1989–2002." *Econ Journal Watch* (7) 1: pp. 4–52.

Judt, Tony. 2010. *Postwar. A History of Europe since 1945.* London: Vintage.

Klamer, Arjen. 2004. "Borders Matter: Why the Euro is a Mistake and Why it will Fail." In *The Price of the Euro,* Jonas Ljundberg, ed., pp. 29–44. New York: Palgrave MacMillan.

Lachman, Desmond. 2010. *Can the Euro Survive?* Legatum Institute.

Larsson, Hans Albin. 2004. "National Policy in Disguise: A Historical Interpretation of the EMU." In *The Price of the Euro,* Jonas Ljundberg, ed., pp. 143–170. New York: Palgrave MacMillan.

Liddington-Cox, Alexander. 2011. "THE DAILY CHART: Portugal's Austerity Impasse," *BusinessSpectator*, March 23. http://www.businessspectator. com.au

Lindsay, Robert. 2010. "ECB in U-turn on Junk Bonds to Save Greek Banking System." *Times Online*. May 4. http://business.timesonline.co.uk.

Ljundberg, Jonas. 2004. "Introduction." In *The Price of the Euro*, Jonas Ljundberg, ed., pp. 1–28. New York: Palgrave MacMillan.

Löffler, Kerstin. 2010. "Paris und London öffnen ihre Archive." *Ntv.de*. November 6. http://n-tv.de.

Maes, Ivo, J. Smets and J. Michielsen. 2004. "EMU from a Historical Perspective." In Maes, Ivo. *Economic Thought and the Making of European Monetary Union. Selected Essays by Ivo Maes*, pp. 131–191. Cheltenham, UK: Edgar Elgar. Published, in Dutch, as "De EMU: De Uitdagin," Ooghe H., et al. (eds.), Samson, pp. 37–99. An abridged draft was published as "EMU from an Historical Perspective" in *The Economic and Business Consequences of the EMU. A Challenge for Governments, Financial Institutions and Firms*, Ooghe H., F. Heylen, R. Vander Vennet and J. Vermaut (eds.), pp. 53–92. Boston: Kluwer Academic Publishers.

Marsh, David. 2009. *Der Euro–Die geheime Geschichte der neuen Weltwährung*, Friedrich Griese, trans. Hamburg: Murmann.

Meyer, Fritjof. 1999. "Ein Marshall auf einem Sessel." *Der Spiegel* 40: p. 99. http://www.spiegel.de.

Mik. 2010. "Mitterrand forderte Euro als Gegenleistung für die Einheit. Spiegel online. http://www.spiegel.de.

Mises, Ludwig von. 1944. *Omnipotent Government: The Rise of the Total State and Total War*. New Haven: Yale University Press. http://mises.org.

———. 1998. *Human Action*. Scholar's Edition. Auburn, Ala.: Ludwig von Mises Institute.

———. 2004. *Interventionism: An Economic Analysis*. Online Edition: Ludwig von Mises Institute. http://mises.org.

Nawratil, Heinz. 2008. *Der Kult mit der Schuld. Geschichte im Unterbewußtsein*. 2nd ed. München: Universitas.

Nazareth, Rita and Gavin Serkin. 2010. "Stocks, Commodities, Greek Bonds Rally on European Loan Package." *Bloomberg*. May 10. http://noir.bloomberg.com.

Neuger, James. 2010. "Euro Breakup Talk Increases as Germany Loses Proxy." *Bloomberg*. May 14. http://www.bloomberg.com.

Ohr, Renate. 2004. "The Euro in its Fifth Year: Expectations Fulfilled?" In *The Price of the Euro*, Jonas Ljundberg, ed., pp. 59–70. New York: Palgrave MacMillan.

Padoa-Schioppa, Tommaso. 2004. *The Euro and its Central Bank*. Cambridge: MIT Press.

Petrakis, Maria and Meera Louis. 2010. "EU Backs Greek Deficit Plan. Papandreou Offers Cuts." *Bloomberg*. February 3. http://noir.bloomberg.com.

Raico, Ralph. 2010. "The Blockade and Attempted Starvation of Germany." Mises.org daily article. May 7 [Review of C. Paul Vincent, *The Politics of Hunger: Allied Blockade of Germany, 1915–1919*. Athens, OH: Ohio University Press, 1985. This review was first published in the *Review of Austrian Economics* 3, no. 1.]. http://mises.org.

Rallo, Juan Ramón. 2011a. "Portugal: Una decada (mal)viviendo del crédito barato," *juanramonrallo.com*, March 23. http://www.juanramonrallo.com.

———. 2011b. "España sí es Portugal," *juanramonrallo.com*, March 29. http://www.juanramonrallo.com

Reuter, Wolfgang. 2010. "German Central Bankers Suspect French Intrigue." *Spiegel.online*. May 31. http://www.spiegel.de.

Rothbard, Murray. 1995. *Wall Street, Banks, and American Foreign Policy*. Auburn, Ala.: Ludwig von Mises Institute.

———. 2000. "Schöne neue Zeichengeldwelt." In *Das Schein-Geld-System: Wie der Staat unser Geld zerstört*, Guido Hülsmann, trans. Gräfelfing: Resch.

Samuelson, Robert. 2010. "Greece and the Welfare State in Ruins." *Real Clear Politics*. February 22. http://www.realclearpolitics.com.

Savage, James D. 2005. *Making the EMU. The Politics of Budgetary Surveillance and the Enforcement of Maastricht*. Oxford: Oxford University Press.

Schäffler, Frank. 2011. "Europäischer Stabilitätsmechanismus (ESM)." *Schriftliche Erklärung*. www.frank-schaeffler.de

Schrenk-Notzing, Caspar von. 2005. *Charakterwäsche. Die Reeducation der Deutschen und ihre bleibenden Auswirkungen*. 2nd ed. Graz: Ares Verlag.

Selgin, George A. and Lawrence H. White. 1996. "In Defense of Fiduciary Media, or We are Not (Devo)lutionists, We are Misesians!" *Review of Austrian Economics* 9 (2): pp. 92–93.

———. 1999. "A Fiscal Theory of Government's Role in Money." *Economic Inquiry* 37: pp. 154–165.

Sennholz, Hans. 1955. *How Can Europe Survive?* New York: D. Van Nostrand Company.

Sennholz, Hans. 1985. *Money and Freedom*. Spring Mills, Pa.: Libertarian Press.

Shortnews.de. 2010. "Umfrage: Mehr als die Hälfte der Deutschen wollen die DM zurück haben." News from June 29. http://shortnews.de.

Sinn, Hans-Werner and Holger Feist. 1997. "Eurowinners and Eurolosers: The Distribution of Seignorage Wealth in the EU." *European Journal of Political Economy* 13: pp. 665–689.

Spiegel.online. 2010."Deutschland weist Bericht über Sarkozy-Ausraster zurück." May 14. http://www.spiegel.de.

Starbatty, Joachim. 2005. "Anmerkungen zum Woher und Wohin der Europäischen Union." *Tübinger Diskussionsbeitrag* no. 292. February.

———. 2006. "Sieben Jahre Währungsunion: Erwartungen und Realität." *Tübinger Diskussionsbeitrag* no. 208. November.

Tagesschau. 2010. "Müss Deutschland noch mehr zahlen?" May 6. http://www.tagesschau.de.

Tarullo, Daniel K. 2010. "International Response to European Debt Problems." Testimony Before the Subcommittee on International Monetary Policy and Trade and Subcommittee on Domestic Monetary Policy and Technology, Committee on Financial Services, U.S. House of Representatives, Washington, D.C. May 20, 2010. http://www.federalreserve.gov.

Telebörse.de. 2010. "EZB öffnet Büchse der Pandora." *Dossier.* May 10. http://www.teleboerse.de.

Teltschik, Horst. 1991. *329 Tage: Innenansichten der Einigung.* Berlin: Siedler.

Thesing, Gabi and Flaiva Krause-Jackson. 2010. "Greece gets $146 Billion Rescue in EU, IMF Package." *Bloomberg.* May 3. http://noir.bloomberg.com.

Tweed, David and Simone Meier. 2010. "Trichet Indicates ECB Bond Purchases Not Unanimous." *Bloomberg.* May 10. http://noir.bloomberg.com.

Ulrich, Angela. 2010. "Ein gutes Geschäft für Frankreich." *Tagesschau.de.* April 30. http://www.tagesschau.de.

Vaubel, Roland. 1994. "The Political Economy of Centralization and the European Community." *Public Choice* 81 (1–2): pp. 151–190.

―――. 2004. "A Critical Analysis of EMU and of Sweden Joining It." In *The Price of the Euro,* Jonas Ljundberg, ed., pp. 87–96. New York: Palgrave MacMillan.

―――. 2005. "The Role of Competition in the Rise of Baroque and Renaissance Music." *Journal of Cultural Economics* 25: pp. 277–297.

―――. "The Euro and the German Veto." *Econ Journal Watch* (7) 1: pp. 82–90.

―――. 2011. "Eine andere Interpretation des Weber-Rücktritts." *WirtschaftlicheFreiheit.de.* February 15. http://wirtschaftlichefreiheit.de/wordpress/

White, Lawrence. 1995. "The Federal Reserve System's Influence on Research in Monetary Economics." *Econ Journal Watch* 2 (2): pp. 325–354.

Wohlgemuth, Michael. 2008. "Europäische Ordnungspolitik, Anmerkungen aus ordnungs-und konstitutionenökonomischer Sicht." *ORDO: Jahrbuch für Ordnung von Wirtschaft und Gesellschaft,* 59, pp. 381–404.

Index